LIBERATING CHOICES

HOW TO LIMIT THE INFLUENCE

OF GOVERNMENT ON YOUR

LIFE AND THE LIVES OF YOUR

LOVED ONES

<u>INTRODUCTION</u>

I live in the coastal region of South Carolina. Years ago, my hometown consisted of a fishing pier, some seafood restaurants, and a few single story hotels. Everything shut down right after Labor Day, and the place was a ghost town from then until the spring thaw.

Today, things are different. The major reason for that is probably the aging of the American population. As the number of retirees increased, so did the number of people with spare time and money in their hands who wanted to make their home, or at least second home, here.

The appeal is obvious. However, when you take the time to speak with your new neighbors, you realize there is something more. Most, if not all, make reference to high taxes, excessive governmental regulation, corruption and crime as factors in their decision. They describe a situation in which the quality of life is depressed by the costs of government, which affects everything.

The complaints are universal and surprisingly consistent. After a while, I began to notice that political affiliations were irrelevant, liberals and conservatives alike said much the same thing. That's not to deny that the liberals, once they moved in, would vote for the same kinds of policies in their new communities that had sent them running in the first place.

As their numbers increased, local government changed. The property taxes increased annually, and each year it seemed that the government discovered new things to tax. The furniture and contents of each dwelling on the beach was required to be declared on an annual tax return, which required each taxpayer to specify, for example; how many trash cans were in the home, the purchase price of each, and when acquired.

The new revenue was like testosterone. Pretty soon, a locality which had been known as the capital of miniature golf, and consequentially had a landscape littered with seemingly hundreds of green plaster dinosaurs was deeply concerned about the size, color, and cosmetics of every sign.

Property owners would postpone making minor repairs to their homes, either to avoid the paperwork, or because of the prohibitive costs. Citizens living on what was obviously farmland, intent on raising their own food, would find it difficult or impossible to plant a crop or maintain a few animals.

These problems are as old as the concept of government itself. It is the nature of an individual in power to use that power, either by creating new rules and regulations, or new methods of enforcement. The founding fathers of this nation saw this and attempted to turn the situation on its head. As Thomas Jefferson said:

> "*A wise and frugal government which shall restrain men from*
>
> *Injuring one another shall leave them otherwise free to regulate*
>
> *Their own pursuits of industry and improvement and shall not take*
>
> *From the mouth of the labor the bread it has earned.*"

There has always been a pressure to increase the reach of government with ever more rules, regulations, and programs. Nevertheless, the principle set forth by Jefferson held fast until far more recently than one might imagine. In nineteen twenty nine, when Calvin Coolidge had just completed his term, the federal government was actually smaller than it had been in nineteen twenty three, when he took office.

Why do I raise this point? If you are reading this, you are probably of like mind to these political thinkers, and therefore part of a dwindling minority. When in 1969, Richard Nixon spoke of a "silent majority" of Americans who thought progressives went too far, he was correct. Since then, however, the country has been subjected to a radical makeover. This is true to such an extent that even so called conservatives no longer speak of eliminating government programs, or reducing the size of government. Rather, they refer to the possibility of reducing the rate of growth.

It is not my purpose here to discuss the economic, political, and social implications of these trends. However, it is at least worth noting that all or part of the rejection of these traditional values can be attributed to certain laziness on the part of those of us who believe in them.

Say what you will about liberals, or as Nixon and Coolidge would have referred to them, progressives. It can also be said of them that they never abandon an idea or policy initiative, no matter how flawed, how farfetched, or how unlikely to succeed. Repeatedly in the past several years, we have seen that dogged persistence pay off, while the mainstream shrugged a collective shoulder and said "That will never happen."

If you disagree with the direction in which this country is going, you have a moral obligation to speak out. The birthright of your children and grandchildren, which is a society that celebrates intellectual freedom, economic opportunity, and privacy rights is at issue. There is a genuine risk that history may look back on our lifetimes as a golden age for the United States and the world, with our descendants unable to even imagine the comfort and opportunity we took for granted.

You are not being asked, as so many of our ancestors were, to risk the ultimate sacrifice in defense of these liberties. In fact, nothing will be said against you if you stand idly on the sidelines and refuse to participate in the process even by voting. At least, nothing will be said for the time being.

Still, if you care about your family, your country, and your loved ones, you must politicize yourself. Set aside the few minutes it might take to learn the truth about political candidates, as opposed to the manipulations presented in their political ads. Check out their voting histories, political affiliations, and past behavior. Once this would have been a difficult to impossible job, now it is easy and convenient.

After the election is over, keep an eye on whoever has been given keys to the hen house. If the candidate you supported has, as is so often the case, begun to behave in a manner different from what was presented at election time, remind your friends and connections on social media. Write e mails and letters to the office holder letting him know that voters in his community are concerned about his or her choices. If you have the time or the inclination, become a voter yourself.

If enough people begin to behave in this way, there could be a change for the better. Granted, the word "change" was to a partial extent co-opted by the current regime a few years ago, with unfortunate results. Still, it is important to keep in mind that what has been done can be undone, especially when so much is at stake and so many are concerned.

In the meantime, you and I must co-exist with a local, state, and a federal government which rules with an increasingly heavy hand. This is so much the case that in fact there has now emerged something of a micro-level of local government, the HOA or homeowner's association. It is surprising but true that the smallest element of government is the one most likely to actively affect your life. Those who ignore local elections, or HOA meetings, do so at their own peril.

As such, this book is intended as a guide for those who, as much as possible, want to minimize governmental interference in their lives. The various choices will be presented with the idea that this is the *primary* concern of the reader above all else. Of course, that will not usually be the case. Nevertheless, the approach has two principle benefits.

The first is that doing so allows us to examine just how extreme government interference in the day to day activities of the average American has become. You might want to stop thinking about this unpleasantness and go fishing. If so, better not do it without a license.

The second is simply to provide a complete answer to the question of "What do I have to do to get the government off of my back?" The ultimate answer, other than obtaining a passport, renouncing citizenship, and commencing a search for an ideal new homeland, is "Nothing." Even if you possess the resources and courage necessary for such a quest, it would be no more likely to succeed than the search for a new husband or wife that follows a forty something mid- life crisis.

On the other hand, the choices you make can cause the situation to get substantially better or worse. You can certainly move to a region of the country in which the laws and public policies are more consistent with your own values. You can behave in ways that make you more or less likely to experience confrontation with government on any level. You can make choices which allow you to be a vehicle of political change.

CHAPTER ONE

WHERE YOU LIVE MAKES ALL THE DIFFERENCE

A few years ago, I represented a man who had moved south from upstate New York. He bought farmland about twenty miles inland, at first intending to tear down the barn and original house and rebuild. After a while, he reconsidered, and decided to repair and modernize the original buildings. He was pleased with the result and for a time enjoyed his new life.

The problem came in the most innocuous of ways. Like many people of retirement age, he and his wife were reading more and more about health and longevity. Concerned about the effects of preservatives and food additives in their diet, they decided to do something about it. The first step was to find a convenient way to add fresh eggs to their daily diet.

Since they were living in the country, and already had a barn, the easiest solution was to raise chickens. They bought several and also one rooster. The man and his wife were both music lovers, and something in its warble and the shape of its throat reminded them of one of their heroes. They decided to call the rooster "Bob Dylan."

Like most animal lovers, by naming the rooster the couple had also created an emotional bond. Bob Dylan became a household pet, more like a dog or cat than any kind of poultry. He slept in the barn, but entered and exited the house as he pleased. He was a proud, and as a rooster will do, crowed proudly each and every morning.

That was the start of the problem. Although their property appeared to be isolated, there was a neighbor living on the other side of a small pond. Unfortunately, the neighbor disliked the morning serenade, which he did not find rustic or peaceful. Rather than cross the pond in his paddleboat, knock on the door, and discuss the situation with his neighbors, he simply called the police.

What followed was a visit from the local constable. The low population, combined with the even lower rate of commercial activity, translated to a very low crime rate. Consequentially, the cops were bored and looking for something to do.

This is one of the ironies of life. Sometimes, especially when a criminal complaint is relatively small potatoes, the alleged lawbreaker is better off in the larger community. It is safe to say that one hundred miles down the road, in a larger city, nobody would have bothered to fire the first shot in what became a war.

It began with a drop by the house. The neighbor was complaining about noise. The homeowner produced the scrawny rooster who was the subject of the complaint, not much here to cause such a stir he explained. The constable asked him to try and keep the noise down, and left.

Two days later, he returned. There had been another complaint. If this continued, he warned, he would write up a citation based on the community noise ordinance. It might be a good idea to remove the offending animal. The homeowner was, as I have said, already much attached to Bob Dylan. He would not be removed from his home.

The homeowner began to do some research as to how to solve the problem. He tried putting roofing shingles around the coop, to dim the morning light. This did not solve the problem. The constable made another visit.

What resulted was a series of TWELVE warrants for violation of the noise ordinance. For evidence, the constable borrowed noise detection equipment from a larger police force that they used during the annual biker festivals. For a period of about ten days, he parked his car across the street from the farmhouse, barn, and coop. At sunrise, he pointed the large, cone like noise detector in the direction of the sound, and wrote in a small notebook.

When all of this finally came before a judge, the neighbor who started it all was nowhere in sight. All that was in evidence was the constable, the noise detection equipment, and the small notebook. The magistrate was amused by the story, but not so much that he intended to allow the case to continue past lunch. The twelve warrants were dismissed because the statute was unconstitutionally vague. That should have been the end of it.

Instead, the constable petitioned the county council seeking to change the zoning of the property to ban farm animals other than certain pets. This passed, but as was pointed out to him, the new law could not be retroactively applied to the rooster in question.

Today, Bob Dylan is still the master of his domain. He holds his chest high, knowing that he is in a category by himself. Not only is he the only rooster in the county, he is the only rooster that will EVER reside legally in the county. It is understandablethat he has something of a swelled head.

Of course, when Bob dies, the homeowners will not be able to replace him or any of the other poultry on the farm. One has to wonder how much this affair cost the county in employee time and

other resources. Alternately, the neighbor might have solved the problem by playing a little light music in the bedroom, leaving a TV on, or just buying thicker curtains to muffle the sound.

There is a moral to this story. When you are choosing a place to live, you need to consider your expectations as to how you plan to live when making your choice. Sometimes, it can be fairly obvious that your intended lifestyle does not fit with the area. For example, if you intend to move into a senior community, and there might be problems with having your grandchildren in the home for extended periods of time.

Other times, the connection can be almost as obvious. I remember hearing a crank phone call once, in which the comedian dialed up a realtor, explained that he had just won the lottery, and said that he was looking for a house in the priciest neighborhood in town. He then began to explain how he intended to spend his time.

"Every now and then we like to butcher a hog," he said, "so the first thing we'll want to do is dig us a good pit in the front yard. You think anybody would have a problem with that?"

"Well," she sounded a bit less giddy, *"You would have to discuss that with the homeowner's association."*

"And another thing," he continued, "We got a big family. We always have company, sometimes twenty or thirty people, especially on holidays. That won't be a problem, will it?"

Her voice was stiffer and much less friendly now. Her dream of a quick, juicy commission was fading fast.

"That would be up to the homeowner's association. If you are not in compliance with their regulations, you can request a variance."

"Thank you. I'll discuss this with the wife and kids and get back to you." Click.

The sad truth is that you don't have to anything remotely outrageous as these plans to be courting trouble. It might be enough to have your house painted in an unusual color, or to construct s storage building or garage, or even to fly an American flag. The possibilities are as endless as the number of thoughts that might cross the mind of a small group of people who have, at least on this small level, seized power.

As much as it might seem otherwise, bickering with a neighborhood HOA can cost thousands of dollars in legal fees. A few of these cases have gone through multiple levels of appeal, to state supreme courts and even to the United States Supreme Court.

Starting at this smallest possible level of government, we come to the question, what is the best way to stay out of trouble with government?

If we are postulating from a time prior to any problem, then the short answer is by carefully choosing your community and neighbors. It is not too difficult to predict how receptive a community will be to your lifestyle, your business, or other concerns. All that is needed is a little planning and forethought.

People have understood this for a long time. I remember an episode of "The Andy Griffith Show" in which a stranger appears in town, and quickly arouses suspicion. He has an unexplained intimate knowledge of the citizens of Mayberry and their personal business. When he attempts to buy a business in town, he is rebuffed. When he asks out a local girl, he is threatened and nearly beaten up by her brother.

Just as he is being surrounded by an angry mob with torches, Andy appears to explain the situation and save the day. It turns out that the stranger had been subscribing to the local newspaper to learn more about the town. His idea had been to find out as much as possible before making his decision to move there.

After hearing this, the citizens of Mayberry adjust their attitude towards the young man. He buys a local business, the girl of his dreams agrees to go out with him, and he presumably lives happily ever after.

This approach would have seemed odd at the time. Now, it is arguably commonplace. We regularly check out potential employees, business partners, and even love interests on line, why not potential new homes of business locations?

It is far easier to do in modern times. Instead of or in addition to the local newspaper, one can learn all there is to know about a community by checking out social media, prominent community web sites, and especially, political postings. The thoughts, values, and habits of any locality are out there to discover. You need only to look.

Beyond that, it is never a bad idea to knock on a few doors before moving into an area. Most people are receptive to the idea of shaking hands with a potential new neighbor and answering a few questions. If you find too many who are not, that is useful information in itself.

There are a few other things that should always be done before making such a momentous decision. For example:

1. Get the crime statistics for the area. It is important to know as much as possible about community safety and the habits of law enforcement. Most realtors will already have this information in hand, or it can be obtained from the local chamber of commerce. If necessary, make a freedom of Information Act request to local law enforcement.

2. Find out what you can about the reputation of the local officials you will have to deal with most. Doing so is by nature more of an art than a science. However, start by doing a Google search of anyone whose cooperation is important to you.

For example, a few years back a client of mine was looking open a restaurant and bar in a new town, but needed a zoning variance to serve alcohol.. He discovered that the county employee who would make the decision had lost a child to a drunk driver, and understandably, had a uncommonly negative view of recreational drinking. This convinced him to purchase an alternate piece of land which did not require the zoning variance.

3. There is always the option of scheduling a meeting with the agency or individual in question. In some circumstances, it can be better to have a proxy handle this for you, such as your attorney or accountant. However well or badly this goes, it will allow you to make informed decisions, which is always important.

Many governmental entities are learning the hard way just how costly it can be to have a reputation as a hard place to live or do business.

For this reason, it should not be assumed that a previously unhelpful attitude towards new business is a continuing policy in a community.

This explains the recent phenomenon of states running ads of TV touting their business friendly policies, or the advantages of living there. It is surprising that many of the states running the ads, such as New York and California, are the last places one would expect to have any problems drawing new citizens or investors. The problem is in the way their governments operate.

If leaving is not an option, and you still wish to live and do business as you choose, there may be no choice but to fight. More on that later.

CHAPTER TWO

HOW TO WORK WITH BUREAUCRATS AND POLITICIANS

A few years ago, Ann Coulter wrote a book called "How to talk to a Liberal –if you must." I won't assume anything about the political affiliations of the person you will be talking to, or even about their inclination or disinclination to help you. Rather, I will present a few ideas that might make any important conversation with a government official, of any kind, a little more pleasant and successful.

At some point, it is a given that we have to divide persons into categories. First, though, a few ideas are sound and important regardless of the situation. Let's examine those.

Most people fail in negotiations because they take the wrong perspective. Instead of focusing on the other person in the room, they approach the process only looking at their own agenda. This does absolutely nothing to increase their chances of success.

Why do people make this mistake? It is primarily human nature. However, more to the point, attempting to do the opposite is HARD. In most cases, you are meeting or speaking with a person you either do not know, or do not know well.

You are probably at least a little uneasy about the prospects of an adversarial encounter with a stranger, and reluctant to think about it. It is much more comforting to reassure yourself by dwelling on your point of view.

At least try to come up with a reasonable idea of what the other person wants. This might be something as simple as a short meeting, after which you go away and never return. It might be a solution to a conflict involving competing interests that he or she has to resolve.

Understanding his perspective dramatically increases the chance of your getting what you want. All you have to do is find a solution that also suits both of your needs, now that you have defined them.

The worst part about it is that, in most cases, your opposite number is not doing the same.

In a general sense, you as an individual have a few inherent advantages when dealing with government. This is the reasons why citizens subjected to an overreaching or even tyrannical government can generally function uninterrupted in day to day life, absent war or other catastrophes, at least.

POINT ONE: YOUR PROBLEM IS ALMOST ALWAYS MORE IMPORTANT TO YOU THAN TO GOVERNMENT.

The first is the fact that the individual will almost always have superior focus to the government entity. This is because the individual has a single problem, and thus a single agenda. The government entity, by contrast, will always be dealing with a huge number of adversarial situations, many of which will be more urgent, more compelling, or more profitable and thus more worthy of attention.

Technology, of course, has reduced this tactical advantage. The information gathering capacity of all levels of government has exploded exponentially in the past few decades, to the extent that it is virtually impossible to maintain privacy. Later on in this book, we will discuss some particulars of this situation. For the present, suffice to say that all of us live in glass houses if only anyone is motivated to look inside. The virtually unlimited access to entertainment, information, and services we have comes at a high price that few contemplate or even notice.

Nevertheless, it is true that through sheer numbers, a face in the crowd is unlikely to be noticed and singled out. As such, the most obvious way of avoiding unwanted attention from any agency of government on any level is to just avoid any action or statement likely to attract attention.

Is this my recommendation as to how you should live? Of course not, this country has a proud heritage of celebrating and defending free speech. The tradition extends from the Founding Fathers who risked life and wealth for the principle, to generations of fighting men and women who far too often gave all in defense of the principle.

The point is raised because the vast majority of situations recommend this as the strategy of least resistance. For many people, and in many situations, the fight is simply not worth the expense. For example, you might be better off to shell out for a fresh coat of paint than to hire an attorney and declare war on your entire neighborhood to defend your color choice.

Sometimes, the principle is more difficult to surrender. The multiple legal challenges relating to the right to fly an American flag at one's home are obvious examples. For the past few years, we have become familiar with the story of the homeowner, often a veteran, who flies the flag at his home, and has run afoul of a local HOA.

For the sake of fairness, it is worth noting that often the objection is not to the flag itself, but rather, to the size of the flag, the height of the pole, or where it is hung. There is an element of urban myth to the extent and nature of this problem. The hugely popular television series "Frasier" even had an episode in which an irate neighbor hangs a gigantic American flag from his balcony to ruin Dr. Crane's view.

POINT TWO: YOU HAVE THE OPPORTUNITY TO OBTAIN SUPERIOR KNOWLEDGE.

Where the principle is too important to simply surrender, there is the second option. Examine the legal authority in question, or hire an attorney to do so, with the idea of searching for a clear legal accommodation.

In other words, look for the loophole.

There is a methodology to this. If you can compel the governing body to identity its exact objection to whatever it is objecting to (in this example, the flag) and *that there are no further objections,* your answer is clear.

To continue with the flag example, you may have received a letter placing you on notice that the property is in violation, and referring to a statute or code provision. If not, you would want to obtain a written document from an individual in authority detailing the violations. This is necessary so that your alleged violation will not become a "moving target", changing every time you attempt to comply.

Once this is accomplished, all that is necessary is to discover the least intrusive, most cost effective way of satisfying the rule. If the problem is that the flag is hanging from the balcony, can it be flown from the porch? If the flag pole is too high, is there a cost effective way to lower it?

This may well solve your problem. If it does not, and you are willing and able to hire an attorney and go to court, it will at least strengthen your case. After a while, if you are still looking for a pea underneath a shell, it will become apparent that the objection is not based upon practicalities, but ideology.

Often the rules and regulations are drawn up in haphazard fashion, to address a particular issue at a particular point in time. When this is the case, loopholes can be vast, and the opportunity to have the last word, or even for revenge, irresistible.

For example, a few years ago snopes.com presented a short article about a disgruntled investor who was refurbishing two homes. The homes in question were located in Cambridge, Maryland. The local building inspector declared them to be non-compliant with historical code.

"Brandon Spear never set out to paint his restored Victorian properties with colors

that were out of the norm. But when local building inspectors told him that the windows

he chose to restore weren't up to historical code, he got angry. "It would have cost

one third of the restoration budget to install those windows," says Spear. Then he

realized the building code said nothing about what colors the old Victorians should

be painted. So as a show of his anger, and as a protest against what he saw as unfair

regulations, he painted one home all black and the adjacent home with an American

theme. They've become something of a tourist attraction since."

Revenge is not only a dish best served cold, but not one that generally benefits the long term interests of the chef. The short term satisfaction of an act like this can be bought at a high price. Nobody likes to look foolish, and anyone embarrassed by a stunt of this nature is likely to hold a grudge. Still, this stands as a stellar example of what can be accomplished by simply knowing the rules, and making intelligent choices within them.

POINT THREE: CONSIDER THE ADVANATAGES OF THOUGHTFUL AGGRESSION

A third rule is to recognize that in some limited circumstances, the individual might actually be in a position to act aggressively.

A word of caution is appropriate at this juncture. Always be aware that you, as the individual involved in a conflict, not an objective decision maker. One of the oldest homilies of the law is that "The lawyer who represents himself has a fool for a client." Do not let your anger or ego persuade you that enemies will run for the hill when you draw your sword. When the enemy is government, with its endless human and financial resources, and minimal accountability, the opposite will usually be true.

However, there are exceptions. They can best be identified by an independent expert who can provide an objective, knowledgeable take on the case. Generally, they involve situations in which there is a clear, documented violation of the law, and some kind of expedited remedy available to those effected.

For example, federal law allows residential tenants to keep "health care" animals notwithstanding a "No Pets" policy in a residential unit. Over time, most property managers and landlords have come to realize that a letter from a doctor stating that the pet in some way fits this description closes the argument.

.   Federal law provides extensive remedies for the pet owner/tenant. Including the possibility of injunctive relief against the removal of the tenant and the animal, as well as an award of actual damages and potentially, attorney's fees, expenses, and costs.

The reality is that few of such cases ever go to trial. The HOA, wary of high legal costs and the serious liability risk involved, will generally be more inclined to simply tolerate the animal in question. After all, the property manager will have to justify this expenditure to the homeowners at election time, who might question his or her judgment.

This can also be the case where the sheer volume of disputes is overwhelming to the governmental entity. For example, in my home county, local government is accustomed to raising the assessment values on vacation homes periodically. Most of the owners reside out of state, and many are elderly and not inclined to litigate.

There is a nature urge to take advantage of the situation, especially since the group is composed of mostly non-voters. Thus, property taxes have become the first choice as a piggy bank to shake whenever additional revenue is needed, or more often, simply desired.

However, others also saw an opportunity, and this has changed things. A few years ago, a handful of local real estate attorney began to place ads local newspapers offering legal representation in tax valuation appeals at affordable, flat fee rates.

What the attorneys knew, and property owners began to discover, was that the number of appeals was rising dramatically. The case load had become far more than the relatively small staff of the county tax assessor could handle.

As such, an unwritten rule of procedure had evolved. For each notice of appeal that was properly and timely filed, the county provided a quick and immediate response. This came in the form of a letter offering to settle the dispute in exchange for a reduction in the increased valuation, usually between twenty and forty percent. Most people were satisfied with that result, even though property values had actually plummeted due to the recession.

POINT FOUR: HAVE REALISTIC EXPECTATIONS AND A DEFINED GOAL. KNOW WHEN TO QUIT.

This leads to the next major rule of succeeding in a conflict with government. Start with a clearly defined goal, and quit when that goal is achieved.

There is always an acceptable outcome and a time in which it is wise to stop. This is true of all things in life, not just legal matters. I remember years ago watching a TV show in which a plastic surgeon was reviewing pictures of Michal Jackson after several of his plastic surgeries. After about the third photo, he studied the reshaped face of the King of Pop, pointed to the nose, and said, "You know this is a really good result. This would have been the place to stop."

How does one make that call? The decision should always be informed by the best information available, interpreted by the most knowledgeable and experienced person available. Usually, the long term value of having the matter resolved properly will justify the cost of an expert, such as a lawyer or a realtor.

To return to the issue of a property tax assessment, a current appraisal of the property would go a long way. This would allow the taxpayer to verify the accuracy other the numbers used by the tax assessor in his calculation. If there is a discrepancy, he or she should also estimate the expenses involved in challenging the assessment, including attorney's fees, expenses, and costs if applicable. The taxpayer should then be able to determine how much of a tax savings must result from the appeal in order for him to actually save money.

In the case of my home county, too many property owners did not know when to stop. As a result, the county began to make the appeals process increasingly more difficult, and sometimes to resort to out and out trickery to cut off appellate rights. For example, last year, the deadline for filing certain property returns was set for the week of Christmas. Presumably, this was intended as a trap for the unwary, as the returns now specified in bold red print that "THERE IS NO PROVISION FOR AN EXTENSION OF TIME TO FILE THIS RETURN."

The county also began to increase the difficulty of simply filing an appeal. The new form specified that the most recent state tax return must be included with the return, along with an appraisal of the property. All of this was intended to discourage appeals by making the process more time consuming and more expensive. The new tactics were successful in reducing the number of appeals, particularly from out of state residents who would be hard pressed to put this package together.

The final option, of course is out and out war, with all issues to be resolved in a courtroom. There are principles worth fighting for, and especially in this day. However, before writing the retainer check to the attorney and firing the first shot, it is important to consider all of the circumstances. Here are some things you MUST do.

First of all, research the history of others who have fought the same battle. This may lead to encouraging news, or at least a valuable note of caution. If you find that the issue in question has been litigated repeatedly, with the same or nearly same result, expect that precedent to repeat itself. This is particularly true if the decisions have been affirmed by appellate courts in your jurisdiction.

If the precedent is favorable, this can be used as a valuable bargaining chip. Seek out an individual who has the power to negotiate, and start talking. Make sure he or she is aware of the legal authority in your favor, and expect good things to happen.

On the other hand, if the legal question has been definitively settled against you, carefully consider whether the fight is in your best interest. If you absolutely cannot walk away from the fight, there may still be better ways to make your point.

First, look at whether there is a political action group which advocates for your position in related issues. If you find one, do everything possible to cultivate this valuable source of information, resources and even financial assistance. Remember, an individual fighting federal, state, or even local government in court is the ultimate David versus an ever more powerful Goliath. Few can afford the costs.

It might be possible to convince a private group to undertake the expense of your case to advance a political cause. This can be a case of having your cake and eating it too. If not, there might at least be the possibility of finding financial relief through setting up a "Fund Me" page, or using some comparable site. It might be that a few people of like mind will stand by you as you fight the good fight.

Alternately, consider whether there is an inexpensive administrative remedy. However, you should keep in mind that most appeals through administrative agencies, where they exist, are inevitably handled "in house" by supervisors unlikely to overrule their underlings.

This makes for an inherently biased situation. Nevertheless, it is possible to obtain a beneficial result in a hearing of this nature. At the very least, it is safe to say that losing an administrative appeal has no effect on your chances of succeeding later in appellate court, and may lead to other advantages.

POINT FOUR: CONSIDER THE POSSIBILE ADVANTAGES OF DOING NOTHING.

Sometimes, the best strategy of all is at some point to do absolutely nothing. In many situations once the initial flurry of paperwork is completed, there is by design a long spell of inactivity. Court cases usually involve two opposing parties; one of whom is seeking to have the court do something (award damages, end a marriage, put someone in jail, etc.) and the other of whom is attempting to prevent that from happening.

When you are dealing with government, time is often on your side. This is especially true with smaller governmental entities.

For example, many small towns derive a substantial amount of revenue from traffic and speeding tickets. Often, the police force and traffic court are small considering the number of cases they have to prosecute. For the system to work efficiently and profitably, it is necessary that the overwhelming majority of cases are resolved in the most cost effective manner. In others word, they

count on the fact that most of the people they ticket will simply pay the fine or negotiate a plea. Otherwise, the system would collapse like a house of cards.

It is also true that in many of these places, police officers are constantly leaving the force and being replaced. The defendants are usually not aware of this, but the local prosecutor certainly is.

This means that requesting a jury trial is a smart move for several reasons. First, the delay creates a window of time in which the arresting officer might leave the force, depriving the prosecutor of his or her key and often sole witness. At the very least, assuming that the defendant did nothing to call attention to him or herself, the delay will cause a dimming of memory for the key witness as well as of enthusiasm.

Secondly, it raises the specter of unwanted expense for the municipality. If your case goes to trial, the profit margin is reduced, even if there is in fact a conviction. For all of these reasons, there will usually be an offer of settlement on terms more favorable than a simple guilty plea.

Many jurisdictions have tacitly institutionalized the process, by passing local ordinances such as the "Careless Operation of a Motor Vehicle," found in my home county. These are intentionally vague, and allow the jurisdiction to pocket a fine, without attempting to convict on a violation which would be reported to the state DMV.

This same approach can be successful even in felony cases. Where a defendant requests a jury trial, and a local prosecutor is feeling political pressure due to a backlog of cases, an opportunity arises. Absent extraordinary circumstances, as a case goes stale, it tumbles down the list of priorities until all involved simply want it to go away.

The prosecutor becomes in effect a motivated seller. The product he is selling is a guilty plea which will move the case off the trial roster. Just like the car dealer with too many units on the lot, he is willing to negotiate.

POINT FIVE: CONSIDER SEEKING THE HELP OF A POLITICIAN

If not for the fact that so many politicians are lawyers, I would believe that politicians exist so that lawyers can avoid being considered the sleaziest people on earth. Granted, the stereotype is not always true, but too often we are governed by dishonest, insincere, and self –serving leaders. The problem of corruption is like a weed choking the life out of our localities, states, and nation.

I just read an excellent book by Peter Schweizer, "THROW THEM ALL OUT: HOW POLTICIANS AND THEIR FRIENS GET RICH OFF INSIDER STOCK TIPS, LAND DEALS, AND CRONYISM THAT WOULD SEND THE REST

OF US TO PRISON." Without borrowing too heavily from his work, he opens with a prescient quote by G.K. Chesterton, written nearly a century ago:

"The mere proposal to set the politician to watch the capitalist has been disturbed

by the rather disconcerting discovery that they are both the same man. We are past the

point where being a capitalist is the only way of becoming a politician, and we are dangerously

near the point where being a politician is much the quickest way of becoming a capitalist."

Schweizer goes on to detail an environment in which elected officials use their influence and insider knowledge for profit, sometimes to a startling degree. He notes that:

"The new crony capitalists...obtain access to initial public offerings on the stock market that can be lucrative. They make their investment decisions and trade stock based on what is happening behind closed doors in Washington. This might entail buying or selling stock based on what they know is going on, or they might "prime the pump" trading stock based on legislation they might have introduced." (Schweizer, pg xvii)

As a result, many elected officials suddenly invest with a genius Wall Street's best can only envy. For example:

"A study in the *JOURNAL OF FINANCIAL AND QUANTITATIVE ANALYSIS* found that U.S. Senators may have missed their calling, they should all be running hedge funds. How else to explain these results based on 4,000 stock market trades by senators:

- The average American investor underperforms the market
- The average corporate insider, trading his own companies' stock, beats the
- Market by 7% per year
- The average hedge fund beats the market between 7% and 8% a year
- The average Senator beats the market by 12% a year

The same point was made by the late, great comedian Richard Pryor in the movie "Brewster's Millions." In the movie, Pryor's character has to spend and completely waste all of a million dollar inheritance in order to win a much larger inheritance. If he fails to do so, he loses all.

One of the things he does in his attempt to waste money is run for public office. His candidacy is based on a "DO NOT VOTE FOR ME" platform. In his first campaign speech, he explains that all of the candidates are crooks. "Why else would we spend all this money for a chance to get elected to a job that pays so little?"

He had a point. Unfortunately for him, the voters recognize the truth in his words, and he wins office. This presents all sorts of new problems.

So why do I mention this? Because, like it or not, it is important that you realize that politics is big business. The idealist who wants nothing more than to serve his or her fellow man falls by the wayside in a system that requires millions in campaign contributions merely to win statewide office. Though, and this is crucial, good people do win office, they are at the very least answering to a group of supports who want and expect to be rewarded for their support.

This leads to a few logical assumptions about what will happen when you ask a politician for help. The first is that:

POINT ONE: THE POITICIAN AND/OR HIS STAFF WILL AT LEAST PRETEND TO CARE ABOUT YOUR PROBLEM AND EXPRESS WILLINGNESS TO HELP.

No matter your station in life, you are of interest to the politician for two obvious reasons. The first is that you are a voter, or at least a potential voter. By taking time out of your life on Election Day, you can help or hurt this person, albeit slightly.

The second is that today, even a mouse can roar. This is primarily due to social media, where a person with hundreds of friends on Facebook or any other social media site can spread the bad word instantaneously and widely.

So, assume you will get empathy. Whether you find anything else is a more complicated question.

POINT TWO: THE CONSTITUENCY SERVICE YOU RECEIVE WILL BE DETERMINED BY TWO THINGS: THE BENEFIT TO THE POLITICIAN AND THE RELATIVE DIFFICULTY OF SATISFYING YOU

Depending on the office, the politician will have a staff of various size and resources devoted to constituency service. Want an autographed picture? No, problem. Want to arrange a tour of

Washington for your church group? Also very doable, and you will probably get an in person handshake opportunity to boot.

The staff of a politician is also a great source for information. For example, if you want to know how to apply for benefits from the Veteran's Administration, there is an assigned staff member for that.

Some things, of course, are more difficult. Your success or failure will depend on your ability to make your problem important enough to act upon. This might be a requirement that takes care of itself, if you are politically active and prominent, a known political ally or someone he or she *wants* as a political ally.

If not, the more people you can make aware of your situation, and who care about your problem, the better. One of the best possible things that can happen is a newspaper or television story about your problem or issue, especially with you directly involved. If you can work a mention of the fact that the Senator, Councilwoman, etc. is aware of the problem and seeking to help, then all the better.

Getting that kind of coverage can be difficult to impossible. The easiest thing to do is to follow up with a letter or e mail, expressing gratitude for the forthcoming assistance, and maybe admiration and respect. Follow up phone calls and e mails on a polite, non-intrusive basis can also have a positive effect.

Social media, again, is important. Politicians monitor these sites for mention of their name, and follow them closely. If your problem is a hot topic with enough people, all of whom know that you are counting on this person for help, it will be noticed.

Keep in mind that if your needs conflict with those of a bigger fish, you become a worm on a hook. This is the way of nature and of politics.

CHAPTER THREE:

AVOIDING CONFLICT

If I were to ask the question, "what does government have?" several things might come to your mind. You might say "money," "power" or countless other things. Chances are that whatever answer you came up with would be correct, unless you responded with "space aliens" "flying saucers" or "mind control devices" and even then I couldn't prove you wrong.

To my mind, the best answer would be "resources." Government has a lot of everything. People, money, real estate, employees, bullets, you name it they got it. Our Federal government in particular might well be the world's single biggest spender, with states and municipalities not too far behind.

Not only that, but government uses all of these resources with little accountability to the rest of us. The vast majority of its actions and expenditures are not even noticed by elected officials, let alone the general public who voted them in. Granted, there may be some hubbub when they do something insane, like providing guns to Mexican drug cartels, but even that settles down after a while.

The point is that, when you come into conflict with government, you will almost certainly be overmatched as far as resources. If the state is out to get you, the odds are stacked heavily in their favor. Fighting city hall has never been easy, but today Goliath has discovered steroids.

Today your whereabouts can be tracked by locating your cellular phone, even if it is turned off. When you walk into a building, a camera is there to document and time- stamp your comings and goings. Your financial transactions are meticulously recorded by your bank, to be turned over to any government agency more or less for the asking.

Government is the biggest, baddest bully in the schoolyard. Government is an NFL linebacker with a bad attitude eyeing your lunch in the playground.

In other words, you don't want to pick a fight. Not only that, you want to do whatever is possible to avoid doing or saying anything that might lead to a fight.

You might think that just going about your business and living a peaceful life is enough to accomplish this goal. If only that were true.

A few years back, a friend of mine needed to raise cash fast. He had been through a difficult divorce, which depleted his savings, and lost his job. To make matters worse, he had been left with a hefty child support obligation, set by a judge who determined his ability to pay based upon the job he had just lost.

He had already sold off most of his belongings, and there was not much left to keep him from going to jail for failure to pay child support. Racking his brain, he remembered a long forgotten asset that promised at least a temporary solution.

His grandfather had left him a collection of rare fish. These were not swimming in the bowl, of course. They were swordfish, caught, mounted, and stuffed decades ago. He had been told that they were valuable and collectible, but had given it little thought until now.

A little research allowed him to identify the species. A few minutes on E-Bay confirmed the fact that they were, indeed, valuable. With no time to waste, he posted his inheritance for sale on line.

The next day the phone rang. The buyer seemed motivated. He wanted to come over to the house right then and check out the merchandise. A couple of hours later there was a knock on the door. That's when things went rapidly downhill.

The caller was from the Environmental Protection Agency. He explained that he suspected that the fish were endangered species, which were illegal to possess or sell. After a few tense moments, he proceeded to impound the inheritance, then prepared and served a warrant.

My client explained that that the items were decades old, and had been in the family for years. The government agent asked if he had any proof of their age or the circumstances. Unfortunately, he had moved several times over the years, and not retained those seemingly unimportant documents.

Still cash strapped, he was caught in the jaws of a dilemma. Not only had he lost the only asset he had with which to pay his child support, and stay out of jail. He now was facing felony charges in Federal District Court.

At this point, it was simply a matter of whether state or federal law enforcement picked him up first. The state family court division could sentence him to up to six months in jail for failure to pay the child support. The Federal charges, as it turns out, had surprisingly stiff penalties.

Amazingly, he was looking at the kind of hard tine usually reserved for drug dealers and other violent criminals. He worried that when he explained why he was in jail, his fellow prisons would not consider him a tough guy who deserved respect.

Due to lack of resources, he was represented by a public defender. Due to the aforesaid lack of proof, she indicated that his defense was questionable and risky. He got what everyone referred to as a "sweetheart deal." Still, he was taken into custody, deposited in federal prison, and became the new cellmate and best friend of a convicted killer.

That was not the end of it. About the time when he should have been released, he was informed that there was a complication as to his release. His home state had held had an arrest warrant for him. This was based upon his failure to appear at a family court hearing, presumably while he was doing hard time over his illegal fish collection. He was in contempt of court for failure to pay child support.

He was transported to a second Federal prison in Kentucky, where he cooled his heels for over a month. In the end, he spent over nine months in jail. What money he had left was completely gone. His possessions became property of the landlord, seized in distress of rent. His girlfriend was long gone.

Keep in mind that all of this havoc resulted from an attempt to sell a few items of E-Bay to raise money.

In a sane world, this could have gone down much differently. Many would question the use of public funds to process this man through the legal system, incarcerate him, then support him in jail. Does this draconian penalty really do anything to protect endangered species, or is it merely a bone thrown to environmentalists for political purposes?

Lastly, what would have been so wrong with just taking away the offending items pending proof of their origin, confirming that the man was not dealing is such goods, and leaving it at that?

With its virtually unlimited resources, and a mathematically impossible number of rules, regulations, and statutes, government is a wild card. Like a bull in a china shop, it wreaks havoc on lives, with little or no accountability for its actions.

This is why business as usual is not enough. Particularly if you own a business or are self- employed, it is important to adopt the right habits and protect yourself.

First and foremost, you need to be aware of what kinds of situations are most likely to lead to a problem. Once you are able to recognize them, it is much easier to step back, plan, and thereby avoid problems. I like to refer to these as "trigger situations."

There are three kinds of trigger events. The first and largest category occurs whenever and wherever money changes hands. We are not, of course, referring to ordinary sales unless you happen to be in a business where the value of each transaction is exceptionally high, such as real estate. Instead, consider situations such as the following:

- Deposits in a financial institution of sufficient size to require reporting to government.
- Loans and loan applications
- Unusually large acquisitions of inventory
- Unusually large purchases or sales

The most outrageous and frequently abused example here is the IRS laws regarding "structuring" of deposits. Banks are required to report any deposit in excess of ten thousand dollars to the Internal Revenue Service. By IRS regulations, a pattern of making repeated deposits of a substantial size but beneath the threshold amount of ten thousand dollars can be considered "structuring."

If the IRS determines that the taxpayer is engaging in the practice of "structuring" this empowers the agency to do a variety of things. Most notably, and shockingly, the agency can seize the deposited funds in question, based upon a presumption that the money must have been obtained through illegal means. This is true regardless of whether there has been any conviction or even criminal charge of wrongdoing.

This has brought about a great number of horror stories. A Michigan grocery store owner was subject to forfeiture of his entire bank account, due to his repeated practice of depositing less than ten thousand dollars at a time. There was a rational and honest explanation. His insurance policy did not cover cash deposits in excess of ten thousand dollars.

Another story told the tale of the owner of a small Mexican restaurant, who had been told by her mother to keep the deposits below that amount "because anything more causesthe bank to have to do extra paperwork." She had never heard the term "structuring" or any of the particulars of this obscure federal law. Nevertheless, over thirty thousand dollars of her hard earned money was drained from her account, without any suggestion that she had committed a crime.

The bank records in question must have looked every bit as innocent as the blank expression on the long dead, stuffed and mounted fish possessed by my friend. Nevertheless, each triggered expensive and destructive transactions with big government for individuals who were certainly not looking for trouble.

Keep in mind that money moving in and out of accounts draws attention. Often the nature of a transaction, such as a real estate purchase, will by necessity require a certain degree of counsel and protection. Other times, such as in the deposit "structuring" cases, the law is set up as a perfect trap for the unwary. When and to what extent you choose to spend money for accountants and financial experts is of course a matter of choice, but however you approach such situations, be aware of the risk.

The second category involves transitions of a different sort. Whenever an individual seeks a right to do something new or different that requires government approval, this results in sudden, heightened scrutiny. Sadly, there a relatively few things that an individual can choose to do that do not require permission from some agency of government. This would include mundane things like adopting a pet, painting your house or going fishing.

Here are a few of the major ones. The list is far from inclusive, of course.

- Applying for a business license.
- Applying for a zoning variance.
- Applying for a building permit
- Applying for a liquor license
- Improving your home or business property

The problem is that by taking any of these actions you are raising your hand and calling attention to yourself . Unlike an increasing number of things, it is not possible to monitor most of these behaviors on line.

Therefore, the individual's best historical defense against overreaching government-lack of sufficient government workers to keep an eye on EVERYONE-still to some extent applies.

A great but fictional example of this occurred in an episode of" Seinfeld". Kramer befriends an elderly couple who owned a shoe shop in his neighborhood, but was on the verge of closing their antiquated business. In attempting to help them, he attracts the attention of a city inspector. The inspector discovers all sorts of building code violations, and demands that the couple make thousands of dollars in repairs in order to remain open.

A similar example occurred in my neighborhood a few years ago when a beach side restaurant closed. More accurately, it was run out of business at the end of its lease. The space was located on a pier with a nice ocean view, and was very desirable. There was soon a hot competition to rent the spot from the city, and naturally, several local political figures saw an opportunity for a quick buck.

Despite interest from a number of sources, the space was quickly given to a group with significant ties to several local politicians. There was a great deal of controversy and public outcry, as the owner of the restaurant which had been forced to close was well liked in the community, which was more than could be said for some of those who had driven him out of business.

Ultimately, the space would end up vacant for over a year, with the city losing thousands of dollars in property and sales tax. The original owner had a business license that predated most of the city regulations, had been "grandfathered in" for this reason, and did not have to comply with the new rules. Nobody had realized that the new owners would have to practically gut the building to put it up to code.

Furthermore, the city had to negotiate a lease which was much more advantageous to the new tenant, surrendering even more tax revenue. The new owners were strangers to the community, as to oppressive cost of upgrades and improvement had driven the original suitors out of the game.

Remember that transitions cause scrutiny by all branches of government. If you intend to occupy a new building or upgrade the old one, figure on expenses for things like new fire extinguishers. If you plan to get into a new line of business, expect all sorts of unwelcome attention, whether or not the new business is welcome in the community.

My third category of "trigger" situations involves controversy or conflict related to your property or business that attracts wrongful attention. This involves things like disgruntled employees, a divorce, the breakdown of a business partnership or generally anything that would cause a former trusted ally to become the worst kind of enemy. Angry people seek weapons with which to do harm. Today, instead of the wrath of God, many invoke the wrath of government.

The contradiction here is that, in order to be happy and fulfilled human beings, it is necessary to trust others. I would not want, nor would I suggest that you, live an empty solitary life acting primarily as a caretaker to your personal wealth. On the other hand, it is only necessary to look around to see that taking some precautions is not only wise, but essential.

If you recognize a "trigger" situation in your life, these are the rules to live by.

1. SILENCE IS GOLDEN: When you think about it, there are few people in your life who need to have intimate knowledge of your problems. People discuss their business to such an extent and to so many people for another reason entirely. They are seeking emotional comfort.

If that is you, try to avoid scratching the itch. Keep in mind just how many people have been convicted on jail house talk, or paid steep alimony based on the testimony of an ex-girlfriend. Even the most trustworthy and loyal people in your life can hurt you, by spreading your story to others, always with slight differences from your original account.

If you have to talk, talk to your lawyer who is paid and required to keep your confidences. Otherwise, get a journal and write down your thoughts. Don't use a computer. The security of your document is never completely secure, and the hard drive will be the first thing anyone who wants to hurt you will look for.

2. KEEP YOUR OWN BOOKS. The fact is that if you own a business, you are a target of bounty hunters. It is common knowledge that the IRS among others gives generous cash rewards for discovering "tax cheats."

This is a point for concern even if you are as pure as the driven snow, and as honest as the tide. As we have seen, the IRS has spent many years chipping away at the standard of proof required for it to safely and legally conclude that an individual is a "tax cheat." There's no need for you to do anything wrong.

The accusation alone subjects you to an extended witch hunt, during which time you could be subjected to the seizure of assets, criminal prosecution, crippling legal expense, and sleepless nights.

The IRS will be discussed in more detail later in this book. For the time being, remember this. It does no harm to keep your important financial records in a safe and secure place. This can be defined as a computer with up to date malware, and a secure password, physically located in a place where third parties, and especially third parties you do not trust, cannot find it.

A secure password would contain at least twelve characters, combining both letters and numbers. Several should be uppercase, not just the first. While you want to use something you can remember, avoid the obvious things such as initials, birthday, etc.

One system that seems to work well is to use a phrase as a memory trigger. For example, "Money is the root of all evil. I want 1,000,000.00 dollars now."

This would translate into a password of "Mitroaeiw1000000.00dn" Unless you tell it to somebody this would be a tall order to crack.

3. TAKE CARE OF MINOR PROBLEMS TO PREVENT MAJOR ONES. Small violations of the law, or things that give the impression of their being small violations of the law, lead to more scrutiny. This principle is relevant on several levels.

The classic example would be the broken tail light that attracts the attention of a police officer and leads to a traffic stop. This, in turn, could lead to a search and seizure of the vehicle, or something far worse. By the same principle, failure to put fresh batteries in a smoke detector could lead to a visit from the fire marshall.

The principle applies equally to your personal relationships. Is your marriage on the rocks? This might be a good time to settle up with your staff on those Christmas bonuses. Otherwise, you face the risk that a motivated individual with a score to settle will ally with your spouse.

4. COMMUNICATE IN WRITING IF POSSIBLE, IF NOT KEEP ALL ANSWERS BRIEF AND RESPONSIVE. This is crucial for two reasons. First, it might become important to be able to perfectly recall what you communicated on a prior occasion at some later date. Secondly, It might be even more important to document what you DID NOT communicate, or to be able to limit your communication to the subjects and responses you want.

This is particularly true with government agencies such as the IRS. The agency has broad powers which enable it to expand an investigation at a moment's notice, whenever an agent sees fit. The audit triggered at a small deduction on your return from five years ago could rapidly morph into a full audit of several years of returns.

In such circumstances, you wish to avoid a personal meeting or phone conversation. However, you also want to appear responsive, cooperative, inoffensive, and uninteresting.

Again, keep in mind that whoever you are talking to also pays taxes, deals with the same government, and might even share all or most of your core values. The best assumption, at least initially, is that this person is doing a job, nothing more. Attacking and personalizing the situation is not only counterproductive, it is unfair.

If you have to agree to an interview, a deposition, or any other kind of open ended interview, there are rules of the game. They were best described by President William Jefferson Clinton, not my favorite elected official, but one I concede to have been considerably smarter than average.

Remember the situation with Monica Lewinsky and the infamous dress? At one point President Clinton (a/k/a "Slick Willie") was forced into a deposition. Later at a press conference he was asked how he had responded to the questions.

One of his strengths was a gift for appearing far less cunning and deceptive than he really was, something as important to a politician as big hands would be to a boxer. In this interview, though, the façade fell away momentarily.

A few minutes into the interview, Clinton appeared to get increasingly angry at the tone and nature of the questions. The smile disappeared, and his eyes hardened. He interrupted a member of the press, and said approximately this:

"These people were asking questions with the purpose of obtaining information to use against me. I answered honestly, but gave minimally responsive answers."

Now, if you have a great memory for the news, you might also recall a few of his responses. Among them were some outrageous, in your face answers such as "That depends on what you mean by using the word "is"". These would be ill advised for anyone who did not happen to be the leader of the free world at the time.

Still, his general response is accurate and very helpful. The truth is that in a deposition or any kind of sworn statement, diarrhea of the mouth is often a fatal disease.

The point is that you are being asked questions by a person whose job is to get information from you which can and will be used against you. Persuading them of the righteousness of your cause, or the unfairness of the situation, is all but impossible. The only real chance of doing that is before a judge or jury, should it become necessary.

So the best response is simply a direct, unembellished answer to the question. If you are asked if your company did business in California in the year 2005, and it did not, simply say "No." Do not mention that it did do business and Nevada, at a location twenty miles from the border. Let the other team carry its own water and do its own work.

There are a couple of other rules for this situation worth mentioning here. The first seems obvious, but failure to follow it has caused problems in most of the depositions I have ever seen. When you do not completely hear a question, or are not sure that you heard it correctly, ask that it be repeated. Better to have someone in the room wonder if you need a hearing aid than to risk a possibly serious mistake in a sworn statement.

The second is a thought about timing and pacing. Keep in mind that, to a certain extent, you have an endless supply of "time outs" during the deposition or statement. If you are tired, nervous, hungry, or just have to go to the bathroom, nobody is going to deny you a few minutes out of the room to regroup.

There may be limitations on just what you can do with the time, however. Under the rules of civil procedure of most states, for example, you cannot discuss your answers with your attorney while the deposition is actually going on.

5. SEEK OUT PERSON WHO HAVE BEEN IN COMPARABLE SITUATIONS, OR INFORMATION ABOUT HOW COMPARABLE SITUATIONS WERE RESOLVED.

History has a habit of repeating itself. For this reason, you want to learn how the governmental entity in question has dealt with people like you in the same or similar situations. This is like battlefield surveillance during wartime. It allows you to plan.

Always take this information with a grain of salt, however. Even as it gets increasingly more difficult to successfully deal with government, there are more and more fish stories out there about getting the best of City Hall. People have always bragged about their charisma, connections, and luck. This is a great opportunity to do so.

6. IF YOU BELIEVE THAT THE "TRIGGER EVENT" COULD LEAD TO AN INVESTIGATION, CONSIDER WHETHER YOU HAVE AN OBLLIGATION TO SELF REPORT.

I am a member of a state bar association. As such, I have an obligation to turn myself in and report any legal malpractice on my part. This may sound ridiculous, but these are old and established rules. The fact is that there is a strong incentive to comply. Whether or not an attorney comes forward and reports his own misconduct is a major factor in the degree of punishment.

The NCAA imposes such a requirement for the university athletic programs it governs. Probably the most frequent examples of self-reporting violations occurs in the context of major college sports, where rules involving the recruitment and handling of student athletes are complex and often counter intuitive.

Many other industries and professions have similar rules. If so, this is something to consider if you are aware of a problem and anticipate increased scrutiny of your business or your activities.

7. NEVER GO CHEAP ON LIFE PRESERERVERS IF YOU THINK THE SHIP IS GOING DOWN.

If you are involved in serious legal issues, seek out the best suited and most capable lawyers you can find and hire them. Do it now. An attorney is like a doctor in that the earlier he or she if brought into a problem situation, the better the chance for a positive result.

I have spent a lot of time, as have most lawyers, talking to people who attempted to represent themselves, either out of dislike for attorneys or to save money. Usually, by the time they realize that they are in over their heads; catastrophic errors have been made which cannot be fixed.

My answer to the question "under what circumstances do you need a lawyer?" is a lot like Justice Holmes' definition of pornography: "You'll know it when you see it."

We'll discuss the screening process for hiring a lawyer later.

CHAPTER FOUR

FAMILY LAW, DIVORCE, CHILD SUPPORT.

ALIMONY AND THE MOST BRUTAL COLLECTIONS

PRACTICES ANYWHERE

Why does family law merit an entire chapter of this book? Because here more than anywhere, ordinary people are caught in the jaws of the big government machine and destroyed.

If minimizing government control of your life is a priority, you should turn and run at the suggestion of marriage and/or children. There is nothing you can do, at least within the law that is a greater threat to your financial stability, freedom, and independence.

This is not to suggest that you should turn the joys of love, parenthood and family. To say otherwise would be an affront to the values upon which our country was built. Of course, that might say more about the current state of American law than anything else.

Family court is traditionally and by definition an area of state law. However, this has not prevented a trend by which these courts have become ever more aggressive in enforcing their decrees. Also, there has been continued encroachment into the area of child support enforcement by the federal government. As defensible as this might be as a matter of public policy, the trend has been towards a shoot first ask questions later attitude when payees get behind.

Still worse for those unfortunate enough to be caught in the pincers, these obligations extend for years or even through lifetimes. Men serve jail sentences for failure to pay support, and shortly after release, are served with a notice to appear in court regarding their back child support. The debt will have increased exponentially during their time in jail.

The obligation can extend past the child's age of majority to pay for college. Where the child is determined, or even alleged to be disabled, the obligation can extend for life.

Likewise, an alimony obligation can extend for years, crippling the obligor financially and draining the very resources necessary to petition the court for relief. Unlike other legally enforced debts, these are court enforced. This means that unlike most judgment creditors, these are the holders of notes that accrue on a weekly or monthly basis, with prompt payment being a condition of the obligor's freedom.

As mentioned earlier, the individual states have the right and responsibility to prosecute child support cases. However, the federal government has taken an increasingly more prominent role in the process.

The federal role crystallized in 1975, when the Child Support Enforcement Program was authorized under Title IV-D of the Social Security Act. Under the current provision, each state runs its own individual child support program. The Federal program assists the state agencies by providing four

major services; locating non-custodial parents, establishing child support obligations, and collecting child support for families.

The program was extended in 1996, when Congress passed bipartisan welfare reform legislation. A top priority of the legislation was to put new muscle into state child support collection efforts.

It is a given that a parent should support his or her child, rather than expecting state or local government to do so. However, a great deal of discretion has been taken away from local trail judges, those best able to discover and act justly upon the unique facts of every case. The result is that in most jurisdictions, the court docket is overburdened with child support cases.

As a result, the unfortunate defendant is given little or no opportunity to address the court and defend themselves. Instead, they are run through a mill and sent summarily to jail.

The new legislation created several new and important enforcement mechanisms. Among these are the national new hire and wage reporting system, the practice of driver's license revocation, and the mechanism for seizure of tax returns. There Federal government has also become actively involved in the effort to locate and track delinquent parents across state lines.

By the year 2000, there had been a sixty five percent increase in the amount of child support collected in the United States. The figure for that year was in excess of eighteen billion dollars, an all-time high.

This is a good thing in many ways. However, practically nobody mentions the fact that the new, get tough attitude is a result of pressure to keep federal funding, not any new interests the plight of the custodial parent and child.

It can be argued that often those parties are injured by this hard ball approach, which makes it difficult or impossible for the non-custodial parent to keep a job. The process also alienates good parents from one another, and in many cases, from the child.

In reality, both parents of a child have a choice to make. They can either involve the government in their lives and that of their child, or not. Those who take the alternate route and go it alone without judge and social worker are in the minority. This is not surprising, as it requires a great deal of mutual cooperation and trust over a long period of time.

Keep in mind that most such arrangements usually fail. Often, the idea is floated by a custodial parent who is concerned about alienating the non-custodial parent from the child. They are correct in appreciating the fact that parental alienation can be tremendously injurious to the development of their child.

However, the youngster also has to eat. The question of whether an informal arrangement for sharing the costs of raising the child will work depends on the nature of the relationship between the parents. I always tell the custodial parent that there has to be a line drawn in the sand.

If the non-custodial parent gets behind in his or her payments by an agreed upon amount, or in excess of a certain number of times, then he or she MUST immediately petition the court for a child support order. If the custodial parent seems unwilling or unable to stick to a hard and fast rule, then he or she should go ahead and file court papers. Otherwise, the result will be economic hardship for the child, unnecessary legal expense, and emotional pain.

That being said, if you are the custodial parent of a minor child, at least consider opting out of the government collections process. If you consider the other parent to be stable, trustworthy, and concerned about the child, it is worth a shot. Just communicate the fact that there is a line in the sand, and that you will not take excuses in lieu of payment.

If you are the non-custodial parent, an informal arrangement has nothing but upside. You avoid being on the government radar, with the threat of going to jail any time you miss a payment, *or the Clerk of Court makes a clerical error.* If there is a true emergency, you have a far more predictable and sympathetic audience to explain your situation to. You may also end up paying less than you would though the court system, since even if the two of calculate the support payment by using the state guidelines you do not pay the clerical fee.

This is why I tell anyone lucky enough to be rearing a child with a parent willing to work with them the same thing. *Be reliable and on time with the payments, and do more when the situation calls for it.* If everyone follows the rules, everybody wins.

The same general principles can be applied to visitation. No court can possibly interpret the changing circumstances and needs of the parents or the child as well as they could be simply communicating. The best chance of allowing a child to have full access to both parents, and enjoy his time with either, is for the parents to work together.

On the other hand, if a regular part of your experience is short notice cancellations or flimsy excuses, you need an enforceable order. Remember, as Thomas Jefferson said, "The government you get is the government you deserve."

Paradoxically, you actually need to go to court over the issue of custody in order to limit government involvement in your family. The reason lies in the effect that uncertainty over the issue of custody might have in an emergency situation involving the child.

Families and marriages break down for a reason. Usually, at least part of it involves a failure to see things eye to eye, to work together, and to respect differing points of view. This problem is never worse than in a crisis.

There should never be a situation in which a parent gets the news that his child is in serious condition at the hospital, and is immediately thrust into a confrontation with his or her ex over who will be making medical decisions. This to me is reason enough to insist that parents who will not be living and raising their children go to court and formalize their custodial arrangement.

So what happens when you fail to do so? At one extreme, the parents might end up forfeiting their authority to the caregiver, who after all has to take some action on behalf of the child. Alternately, the standoff can trigger a situation in which decisions would be made from the bench, with the advice of a court appointed guardian.

There are other reasons why there must be a legal document defining the relationship between the child and the two parents, as soon after they separate as is possible. There are commonly disputes between the parents over the tax deduction related to the minor child. Often, the parents file separate returns, each using the deduction, and trigger audits of both returns.

Another flashpoint area relates to educational issues. Naturally, the child's school will want to know who has physical custody of the child. In fact, even if there is no court order, many school districts will essentially force the parents to designate a custodial parent for emergency purposes.

For the same reasons, it is also wise to have a validly executed will that designates who would take custody of a minor child should the custodial parent, or both, die suddenly. Otherwise, the decision is left in the hands of the state and resolved by a probate judge or a social worker. In the best case scenario, with the most competent and caring individual possible handling the matter, your child's best interest is still left in the hands of a perfect stranger.

There is good news and bad news as to the issue of alimony. The good news is that there is a downwards trend as to the frequency and amount of alimony awards. Chances are that, unless you are involved in a marriage of considerably longer than average duration, have a spouse who is economically dependent on you, and are at fault in causing the breakdown of the marriage (Think adultery/abuse) the chances of an alimony award against you are slim.

The bad news is that the possibility still exists, and when it happens, can have the effect of a wrecking ball on your life. It is common for an alimony award to be permanent, unlike a child support obligation which usually ends when the child reaches the age of majority.

Still worse, the cases that produce alimony awards tend to be bitter, acrimonious, and mean spirited. The cash award becomes more than just lifestyle insurance; it is also a tailor made vehicle for revenge. The pain never has to end as long as the court proceedings go on.

The second best way to avoid this trap (the first is to not get married) is a solid, well executed pre-nuptial agreement. This is something you should not even consider preparing on your own. While most state courts will enforce the contract, this is only true if the document meets certain criterion and if adequate financial disclosures have been made to both parties. An attorney experienced in family law should prepare the agreement and preside over all steps in its execution.

You may find that your soon to be spouse is less than receptive to this idea. From my experience, this is less frequently the case than it would have been a few years ago. However, if you find this to be a hard sell, keep at it, especially if there is a large disparity between your economic status and that of your future spouse. If he or she absolutely refuses, carefully consider whether or not you are willing to go on faith and choose love. Marriage is not a Lifetime Channel movie and the percentage of marriages that end in divorce is astoundingly high.

As I am writing this, the United States Supreme Court has just legalized same sex marriage. It can be fairly said that this is a tremendous societal change, for better or worse.

However, the most significant aspect of the case has been little commented upon. Historically, family law, including areas such as divorce, child custody, child protection, and the like, has been an area in which authority has been reserved to the individual states and their courts.

This opinion becomes the first instance of the Federal Court system grasping control in this area of law. What will be the long term significance? Once can only make educated guesses. However, an increase in the frequency of alimony awards, a national child support system a uniform support guidelines, and a streamlined and more aggressive procedure for enforcement, are among my expectations.

CHAPTER FIVE

IF YOU ARE ARRESTED

The area of criminal defense law is not the focus of this book. There is a mountain of literature on the subject, so much that the problem for the curious is deciding what not to read. Besides that, if you are charged with a felony, the constitutionally guaranteed right to counsel applies, so you WILL have an attorney.

Nevertheless, there is one area of criminal law that needs to be discussed. Otherwise, this book would feel incomplete, particularly in light of current events. Most Americans will find themselves under arrest at some time in their lives, even if just briefly due to a traffic offense. What happens in that brief period of time will probably be the most significant contact with government you will ever face. Far too many Americans are seriously injured or even killed at the hands of law enforcement.

The problem is serious and getting exponentially worse. A vicious cycle has arisen by which the general public has lost trust in law enforcement. Instead, an attitude of distrust, fear and hatred has been created. The result has been a sharp increase in acts of violence towards law enforcement officers. This, in turn, has caused more aggression towards criminal defendants and the general public.

It does not help that our federal government has been busily working to militarize your local police force. Check out the web site for your local sheriff or police department. You might be surprised at some of the heavy artillery they proudly display, much of it slightly used for desert warfare. Nothing about this trend has the effect, or is intended to, put the citizen at ease. Rather, there is a tone of intimidation.

On the opposite end of the spectrum, law enforcement has also been provided with new tools that are less lethal, but dangerous and painful nonetheless. The Taser for example has become a favorite toy. Police are taught that the Taser is a harmless albeit painful way to take control of situation or person. Consequentially, many officers will use the thing at the drop of a hat.

The truth is that the severe electrical shock it generates is a severe health hazard. There have been several deaths and countless serious injuries as a result of use. There is a serious disconnect between the realities of the situation and the attitude of many police; and certainly between that attitude and the feelings of the public they exist to serve.

A recent CNN story "Are Tasers safe?" described how the device works, quoting the results of a study by Dr. William Bozeman:

"Typically a Taser can pack 50,000 Volts, when it actually makes contact with

a person 1,200 to 1,300 Volts pulse through the body. A shock of just a half

second causes intense pain and muscle contractions. The manufacturer says

that recovery is instantaneous and long lasting side effects are rare."

The article goes on to note the results of a study finding few serious injuries as a result of the use of a Taser. Tellingly, it does note that more serious injuries result from "falls following the use of the device." Still more tellingly, the study in question was funded by the National Institute for Justice, a group with a clear agenda in favoring use of the device.

However, the article ominously notes that "Amnesty International found that 245 people in the United States have died from cardiac arrest after being shocked with a Taser. Amnesty and other groups have called for further investigation into how dangerous these devices may be.

Often the devices are being used in incidents in which no arrest occurs. This is not surprising, in that officers are being told that the device is harmless. Should you be concerned about a confrontation with an individual armed with such a device and given a green light to use it? You be the judge.

You are defective car tail light away from such a confrontation. How you deal with the police officer in question has everything to do with whether you get out of the situation safely, and whether or not you are charged.

As in any other communication with a stranger, the more you know about the person you are dealing with, the better the result will be. In general terms, a law enforcement officer has some of the same attitudes one would expect from a judge. That is to say, they place great value on their status as members of law enforcement.

I do not mean to imply that this is necessarily a bad thing. If it were not the case, it would be even more difficult to find people willing to sign up for a dangerous, life threatening, and underpaid job that is essential to the survival of our society.

Like them or not, without the police, your loved ones, your property, and your life are at constant risk. Consequentially, your ability to deal with any of your other needs is severely compromised. You need only to turn on the news to see what happens when law and order fail in a community.

A good start is to be aware of how to properly address an officer. When in doubt, it is safe to simply address him or her as "officer." It's difficult to imagine an officer becoming angry with a member of the general public for being unaware of their rank structure, or supervisor.

However, here are some hints about how to address an officer appropriately:

OFFICERS: The vast majority of personnel seen on the street will be "officers." Their uniforms are unlikely to have stripes or shoulder brass. This is not standardized, but veteran officers might have stars on their sleeves.

CORPORALS: Will usually have two stripes on their sleeves. Often, detectives have the rank of corporal, so an officer you might see out and about in business attire might fit here.

SARGEANTS: Usually three stripes on the sleeve. They are in the field sparing due to administrative duties.

LIEUTENANTS: Brass bar on each shoulder. They are in the field even less than Sergeants.

If you can remember these general rules, you them in addressing the officer. It shows respect, and also might make him or her wonder if you have a law enforcement or military background, which cannot possibly hurt.

Beyond that, be aware of the rules of the expectations of the arresting officer. First and foremost, the officer is concerned with evaluating you as a potential threat to his or her safety.

A traffic stop is the most common scenario. Using it as an example, you would begin by slowing down and signaling to pull off the road immediately after seeing or hearing the siren. If at all possible, be sure to pull far enough off the curb so that the officer can approach your car without standing in the road. I have heard numerous police officers related that drivers who fail to do this anger them immediately.

Wait in the car for the officer to approach. If your vehicle registration and proof of insurance are in an easily accessible folder in the glove compartment (and by the way, they should be), have them ready.

If you are going to have trouble finding them, wait for the officer. The last thing you want to be doing when he approaches is fumbling through the glove compartment. He might respond by pulling his gun.

From there, let the officer talk. He will explain why you were pulled over, just wait for it. This is not the time to argue your case, unless he invites you to explain. There will be an opportunity to do that later, before a judge or jury. Keep your calm, and save any venting you might need to do for later, when you are among family and friends.

A golden rule for this situation is the always allow the officer to see your hands. Ideally, you would rest them on the steering wheel or anywhere upwards, within his clear line of sight. As long as he can see that you are not reaching for anything, he feels safe. The safer he feels, the safer you are.

If you have to reach for something, communicate. For example, if the officer asks for your registration, and it is in the glove compartment, tell him that you will have to look in the glove compartment before actually doing so. Likewise, if you have a gun on board, it is better to advise him of this fact up front. (Your gun permit, of course, should also be included in the folder with the other paperwork in the glove compartment.)

If the officer requests the right to search your vehicle, you have certain options. If there is nothing in the vehicle which would suggest any violation of the law, you might want to consent. However, keep in mind that your definition of safe, legal and harmless might conflict with the interpretation of the public servant currently servicing you.

If not, you can refuse. This will not absolutely solve the problem, but will require him or her to tow the vehicle, and get a warrant in order to make the search. The search warrant can be issued by a local magistrate.

In practice, the local magistrate will ALWAYS issue the search warrant. However, to get the warrant, the officer will have to show that there is probable cause to believe that the search could yield evidence of a crime. This at least makes it possible to challenge the legality of the search later, if you are charged with a crime.

`If you are asked questions, your answers should be short and responsive. Keep in mind that the officer will take notes and file an incident report, so you do not want to say anything that can be thrown back at you in a trial. It is generally a good idea not to discuss your guilt or innocence as to any potential charge, as the officer has probably already made up his mind to charge you at this point.

Chances are that you will then be given a ticket, and allowed to go on your way. Looking at this form the perspective of an arrest, if you have not compromised your ability to defend the case in court, and have not been harmed in any way, you have handled the situation well.

The odds that anything worse will happen are still minimal. The outrageous incidences which are receiving so much attention in the media are noteworthy primarily because of their scarcity. If federal, state, and local law enforcement were making in common practice to batter, abuse and murder citizens, this would be impossible to conceal in our modern times.

The principle reason for this is the cameras that have sprung up like weeds everywhere. One of the more unexpected developments of our recent history is the importance of the digital camera, everywhere and in the hands of everyone. Soon, there will be drone aircrafts filming us from the sky on a constant basis. The images they record will become the final word in every dispute.

For now though, the task of documentation rests with the general public. Arrest footage, filmed by bystanders, has become the smoking gun in many police abuse cases. Beyond all doubt, the practice has advanced the cause of justice. However, it is also true that in many cases the footage can be deceptive, because it puts events out of contexts, or omits.

Regardless, if you are in the habit of using your phone camera for this purpose, or feel the need to do so, you should be aware of your general rights. The American Civil Liberties Union published an article in July 2014 that addresses this issue **"KNOW YOUR RIGHTS: PHOTOGRAPHERS."**

The information it contains can be summarized as follows:

When in public spaces where you are lawfully present you have the right to photograph anything that is in plain view. That includes federal buildings, transportation facilities and the police. This is a form of governmental oversight which has been respected almost from the birth of photography.

When you are on private property, the property owner may set rules about the taking of photographs. There may be valid reasons why a property owner might want to restrict or deny access. For example, many museums forbid visitors from photographing art exhibits, due to the damage that flash photography can do to the works of art over time. In fact, the privacy interests of the person in his own image or that of his property is sufficient to permit legal restriction.

Police officers may not confiscate or demand to view your digital photographs or video without a warrant. The Supreme Court has ruled that police may not search your cell phone when they arrest you, unless they obtain a warrant. I agree with the ACLU that the United States Constitution broadly prevents warrantless searches of your digital data. It is possible that warrantless searches might be legally valid under certain exigent circumstances, such as to prevent the destruction of evidence or save a life. Exceptions of this nature in search and seizure law have tended to become broader and wider over time, like a river cutting through rock. Stay tuned.

Police may not delete your photographs or video under any circumstances. Officers are subject to felony charges for evidence tampering, obstruction, or theft, just as a private citizen would be.

Police officer may legitimately order citizens to cease activities that are truly interfering with legitimate law enforcement operations. The distinction between monitoring law enforcement activities, which you have an unquestioned constitutional right to do, and "interfering" with them is subtle and being worked out by the courts. Cross the line at your own peril.

Note that the right to photograph does not give you the right to break other laws. For example, if you are trespassing to take photographs you are still breaking the law.

This does not mean that inserting yourself into an arrest situation is safe or even smart. There have been numerous incidents in which a police officer has taken a camera by force, impounded or even destroyed it. As with many other situations, the fact that you have a right does not mean that every person you deal with will respect that right. If you involve yourself in a situation of this kind and end up in a lawsuit, chances are that you and your loved ones have been impacted in a serious way.

CHAPTER SIX

KEEPING THE GOVERNMENT FROM

DESTROYING YOUR SMALL BUSINESS

The irony is that, to some extent, the way to prevent government from harming our even shuttering your small business is to reach out, not avoid, government. This is especially true for small business when dealing with local government.

Up to a point, a great deal of trouble can be avoided by creating an atmosphere of informality and trust. You are unlikely to be able to pull this off with, say, the IRS, but local Tax Commission might be an entirely different matter.

For example, a few years back the wage withholding figures for our employees were consistently a few dollars off. This would trigger a response from an agent of the Tax Commission, who would request that we reconcile the forms. The discrepancy was minor, but as any bookkeeper would know, that does nothing to solve the problem.

After a while, our conversations became a little less formal. He was a perfectly nice guy who happened to be a big college football fan, and we had some friends in common. Did this mean that my problem was solved?

No. However, there was a significant improvement in the situation. The first few times, he had sent an ominous looking envelope containing a subpoena, requiring me to appear with the documents about five days from the date on the envelope.

This was playing havoc with my schedule, which involves clients who wait a long time to go to court, and are not happy when things are postponed. After we broke the ice, it became a matter of simply calling him up, telling him that I got the paperwork, and letting him know that my bookkeeper would call. He was fine with that, since he already knew that I was taking the problem seriously and would keep my word.

Will I always be that lucky? Chances are that most of my run- ins with local, state and federal government will be lot less friendly. The faces of the state change incessantly and as those changes go, so goes your relationship with the governmental entity. You may be the most straightforward, honest, and meticulous person imaginable, but with enough contact, you will eventually find a problem.

Therefore, regardless of the circumstances, the idea is to limit the number of contacts. This is the best way to survive in the long run.

Some of my suggestions here will conflict with other principles, and possibly even what you might see as the mission of your business. However, my advice is intended to answer a single question, which turns out to be an ever more important. How do I limit government involvement and consequential interference in my life?

The first principle is to as much as possible; minimize the number of employees in your business and particularly the number of full time employees. The reasons are obvious. As the number of employees increase, major new obligations such as worker's compensation and Obama care kick in. They insinuate themselves into the bottom line, swelling the overhead exponentially and making it increasingly difficult to survive.

Some of the effects of increasing staff are less obvious. For example, depending on the state, there is a number at which anti-discrimination laws apply to a business. Most often, this occurs at about half a dozen employees. Such laws might seem unimportant until the first disgruntled employee receives a pink slip and declares war.

A great many services can be referred to independent contractors at a cost effective and convenient basis. If you are considering this option, there are a few things you should know.

Most importantly among them is to have a good idea of just what an independent contractor is. The definition is strict, and you can expect such work relationships to be carefully examined. This is because government at all levels dislikes independent contractors, for the same reason you should love them.

That being said, the definition of an independent contractor is defined by the Internal Revenue Service as follows:

People...who are in an independent trade, business, or profession in which they offer their services to the general public are generally independent contractors. However, whether these people are independent contractors or employees depends on the facts in each case. The general rule is that an individual is an independent contractor if the payer has the right to control or direct only the result of the work and not what will be done and how it will be done. The earnings of an independent contractor are subject to the self-employment tax.

This definition comes from the IRS web site and is current as of June 30m 2015. As the language suggests, there is a tremendous amount of litigation as to just what satisfies this criterion in a specific situation.

The cases have generally been resolved based upon the degree of employee control. The IRS publications on the subject, particularly Publications 15-A and 15-B, suggest that the employer review the following aspects of the relationship:

1. **Behavioral:** Does the company control or have the right to control what the worker does and how the worker does his job?

2. **Financial:** Are the business aspects of the worker's job controlled by the payer? (These include things like how worker is paid, whether expenses are reimbursed, who provides tools/supplies, etc.)

3. Type of Relationship: Are there written contracts or employee type benefits (i.e. .pension plan, insurance, vacation pay etc.) Will the relationship continue and is the work performed a key aspect of the business?

The best time to be thinking these questions through is before entering into a business relationship with the provider. If you intend to have an ongoing pattern of sending business to an essential provider, enter into a written contractual agreement. It should specify all of the essential elements of the working agreement, and thus, the independent nature of the contractor.

If you in fact have some financial interest or control in the second business, it may be problematic to claim independent contractor status. It would be wise to obtain the advice of a tax attorney and/or CPA.

Regardless, it is beneficial that both entities exist in a corporate form. The bottom line is that a business, and by extension a contractual relationship between businesses, is defined by the identities of the players. Therefore, we start to prove that a service provider is independent of a second business by giving it a unique and independent form.

When you successfully arrange an independent contractor relationship, you obtain numerous advantages. You avoid the need to pay benefits to employees, to file withholding and other governmental compliance forms, possibly to obtain health insurance or workers' compensation insurance, and also avoid certain potential liabilities.

Not the least of these is negligence liability in tort law. The independent contractor is not your agent or employee, merely a third party performing a task for hire. Therefore, you have no liability in civil court for its negligence or even intentional acts should they damage a third party.

You might have an investment or even managerial role in the independent contractor, but keep in mind that this area of the law is steeped in shades of gray. The more hands on involvement you have in the independent contractor, the more at risk you are should the IRS or state tax agents scrutinize the relationship.

This relates to another crucial point. Your business absolutely must exist in one of several corporate forms. The cost of incorporation is minimal, and the advantages are outstanding.

First and arguably most importantly, incorporation allows you to select the home state of your choice, even if it is not the principle site of your business. This, to some extent, permits you to choose the state laws which will be applicable to you. The differences can be dramatic in relation to corporate taxes, shareholder disputes, and the like.

No small factor in the decision is how "business friendly" a state is reputed to be. As government has become more activist in the past few decades, there has been a steady flow of small business and with it jobs and revenue, out of certain states. This is why you see states such as New York and California, who once had no problem in this area, running television ads attempting to lure business owners back over the border.

By contrast, there is a long tradition of businesses incorporating in Delaware. This is because the common and statutory law of that state has been, almost from the start, created with intent to protect and nurture business.

As to the corporate forms, they are consistent in every state. As a practical matter, there are only two from which most businesses will choose. While they share common advantages, there are important differences worth discussing.

The "C" corporation is the classic and original form which extends historically through our common law. It set forth all of the original elements of the corporate form; perpetual life and unique identity from its owners and investors.

The form has two principle advantages. The first is that it is, in the eyes of the law, literally a person in its own right. The corporation can enter into contracts, pay taxes, even be prosecuted for a crime. This is useful because when things go wrong, the corporation can serve as a liability shield for the individuals who own and operate it.

This is why the form is essentially to business investment. With the advent of the corporation, a person could put money into a venture and be assured that the only thing he or she risked was the actual money invested, not his or her entire net worth.

Relative to the relationship between government and business entity, this protection is incomplete, but still substantial. Directors and officers of a corporation have substantial protection from civil and criminal liability. The larger the corporation the stronger the protection, since it relates to the extent of actual knowledge and participation in any wrongful act by the director. Still, the fact remains that even a smaller corporate entity serves as something of a shield against civil and criminal liability.

The "C" corporation, however, does have one major disadvantage, which exists for precisely the same reason that produces the wonderful liability shield. Because it is considered a living being in and of itself, it is unfortunately also treated that way for tax purposes.

This has two unfortunate results. The first is the fact that a separate tax return is required for the corporation, and consequentially still more lost resources related to bookkeeping and accounting.

The second is worse. When the corporation pays out its profits to the shareholders, this is considered a taxable event. As a result, every cent of profit from the venture is taxed TWICE, once when it is earned by the corporation, and a second time when it is paid out to the shareholders.

The Limited Liability Corporation was created specifically to change that. Small businesses were unable to claim the advantages of the corporate form because of the tax consequences. To address this concern, states cases Limited Liability Corporation (LLC.) statutes.

These resolved the double taxation issue by providing that in an LLC. distribution to investors and shareholders is not a taxable event. This is why the overwhelming majority of small businesses are formed as LLCs.

However, there is one major disadvantage to the form. Unlike a "C" corporation, an LLC does not exist perpetually. While the designated life span differs from state to state, inevitably, an LLC will expire and cease to exist. This is not a problem, provided that the owners are diligent about re-filing the necessary paper. If not, the advantages of the corporate form, including limitation of civil liability, cease to exist with the corporation.

Chances are that incorporating your small business is in your best interest. Likewise, it is highly probably that the ideal form for the business is an LLC. This is a crucial step best taken with the advice of an attorney and a certified public accountant. I strongly suggest obtain the best expert advice possible.

I would not have so ten years ago, but you are often better off to rent business property as opposed to buying. The principle reason for this is the bad economy. Simply put, the rental market in many places is a buyer's market, with great deals to be had.

However, there are also substantial benefits relative to your relationship with government. First of all, you avoid paying property tax. Sure, the taxes are incorporated into the rent, and the tenant pays them in the end.

Still, you avoid the nuisance of filing an annual property tax return. This is more of a benefit than you might think. In many areas, these returns ask for information as minute as the year, month, and price for each item of furniture inside the building. There is also the annual need to monitor the valuation used in your locality to determine the tax, so as to avoid being robbed blind. .

You also retain flexibility as to your location. There is real value to freedom, especially when a governmental entity becomes interested in your business activities, whatever the reason. At the very least, rent property first, while you get to know your locality and your customer base. Look to purchase later, if things go well.

Since you are unlikely to be responsible for repairs on a commercial lease, you avoid the hassle of maintaining tax forms for every contractor you hire. All of these things add up to waste your time or employee time. That translates to money out of your pocket.

You might also consider leasing an automobile for your corporation. The lease payments are deductible, and there can be a substantial tax savings. Most people find that maintaining daily mileage logs is a nuisance and lose the habit in time. The deduction is also an audit trigger, so be forewarned.

A major question that comes up on a daily basis is "in what form should you pay the bills?" For all the alleged convenience of credit and debit cards, the old fashioned way is still the best.

You won't turn on your TV and see commercials touting the wonderful benefits of paying for things with money. That doesn't mean that they don't exist. They include among other things:

1. There is no risk of identity theft.

2. There is no interest charged to you.

3. There is no third party billing you and reporting to a credit agency.

4. There is minimal paper trail.

For the time being, currency is still legal tender in this country. One has to fear for the viability of the dollar in light of current events, and worry about its capacity to sustain value. I am no economist, but it makes good sense to say that, if you happen to have a substantial amount of cash, it might be wise to use it now.

As was mentioned earlier, there are risks to making large purchases or substantial bank deposits in cash. Legitimate transactions can trigger an audit, result in seizure of your assets, or land you in jail. The IRS rewrites its regulations perpetually, so the trigger point at which such transactions are reported by your bank is a moving target. This is another area in which diligence and expert advice is important.

When you pay cash, organization and documentation is crucial. Get into the habit of keeping every receipt and scanning it into a computer on a daily basis. About the only disadvantage of paying with cash is the fact that so many people lose receipts. This can become an expensive habit.

Alternately, there are times in which you want a paper trail, and are willing to pay for it. In such cases use a debit or credit card, or a check. Of the three, the check is probably the most secure option. As long as a theft is reported in a timely basis, the bank from which the funds are drawn has little choice but to reimburse the depositor. It is much more in the comfort zone of most thieves to take an active credit card number and simply start spending.

CHAPTER SEVEN

THE HOMEOWNER'S ASSOCIATION

(YOUR FRIENDLY NEIGHBORHOOD TYRANT)

The Homeowner's Association is a relatively new concept which has grown exponentially in the past few decades. These were a rarity not too long ago, mostly found in resort areas where property owners generally lived far away and needed a method for doing business. According to one source, in the 1960's there were only about 500 HOA's in the United States.

Today, they are everywhere. The Community Association Institute estimates that 62 million US residents live in 309,600 HOA communities. So what is a Homeowner's Association (also referred to as simply an "HOA") It can be defined as follows:

An organization made up of neighbors concerned with managing the common areas of a subdivision or condominium complex. These associations take on issues such as garden, pool, and fence maintenance, noise abatement, snow removal, parking areas, and dues. The homeowner's association is also responsible for enforcing any covenants, condition, and restrictions that apply to the property.

(Nolo's Plain-English Law Dictionary)

This all sounds well and good, even necessary. In fact, your property values to a large extent depend on the condition of common areas adjacent to your home. It seems only fair that everybody chip in and contribute equitable towards this mutually beneficial goal. Am I right?

Yes, up to a point, and my expressed reservation is an important one. There are two major areas of concern here. The first is that most people do not appreciate the fact that, when they buy into a property with an HOA, they are essentially pledging citizenship to a tiny government.

This means that you are subject to the tyranny of the majority, or even worse, the minority. This is possible because, in most HOA's, ownership of units equals votes. Therefore, if there is one majority owner of the unit or the development, he or she can dictate policy.

For example, a few years back I had a client who owned a single unit in a beach side complex. The property values had plummeted, and it was easy to see why. The place was strewn with weeds, the grass was knee high, and the common buildings all needed a coat of paint. I was driving through the place in July, at the peak of the tourist season, when everything should have been polished to a high sheen.

It turned out that one guy, who resided out of state and seldom visited the area, owned about sixty percent of the property. So with all that money tied up in the property, why wouldn't he want it maintained? Apparently, the majority owner had run out of funds and was cash strapped.

Unfortunately for my client, he had elected himself as president of the HOA. He voted down any proposal of a special assessment to repair and maintain the common areas, but that was the least of it.

He aggressively pursued any other homeowner who failed to pay HOA dues on a timely basis. However, from the time of his election, he ceased paying them completely.

Not surprisingly, he was a lot more forgiving when it came to his own dead beat status. The once highly desirable complex was falling apart. Local realtors and attorneys were aware of the situation, and the condominiums were slowly becoming unmarketable.

My client was examining the possibility of filing suit against the majority homeowner. It was obvious that something had to be done. Unfortunately, the lawsuit would be time consuming and expensive, and the outcome uncertain. I suggested that he organize a meeting of the minority members, to ask for their support, financially and otherwise.

Everyone of course, was willing to cheer him on, and eager to testify. However, when it came time for the offering, they were less enthusiastic. Only a few property owners offered to contribute to the substantial expense of funding a lawsuit. As it turned out, a major reason for this was the fact that the majority owner had experienced something up an upswing in his fortunes. He was offering to buy them out, albeit at a fraction of what the units had previously been worth.

This situation is a work in progress, so I cannot report an end result. However, it shows that the old saying about absolute power corrupting absolutely is just as valid when the kingdom is a condominium or apartment building as when a nation.

So how do you protect yourself? For openers, in many situations, you do not need an HOA. If you are looking at a home in an established residential area, without shared amenities, and the property looks to be acceptably well maintained, there may be no need. The homeowners will have a common interest in keeping their properties up to a certain level, and will probably take care of the basics such as landscaping, etc. The same principle would apply if you are looking at property in rural areas.

In either case, if you are looking at multiple properties, and one has an HOA, consider this a reason not to purchase. Even if the HOA dues are relatively low, and the association appears benign and hands off, that could always change.

So what if you have already bought into one of these kingdoms? As with any other conflict, the odds of success increase dramatically with your level of preparation. As such, the first thing you need to do is your homework.

Therefore, **know the rules and bylaws.** If you have not done so already, obtain a copy of the rules, covenants, by laws, and deeds. Review them carefully, and if necessary, have them reviewed by your legal counsel. What you find may surprise you.

You can count on the fact that the deeds and covenants are prepared by lawyers. As to anything else, this might or might not be the case. Consequentially, there might be some real surprises in the by-laws, which can be arbitrary, illogical, and downright unfair.

Again, it is always possible to take the HOA to court. However, this is time consuming, and expensive, and success is not guaranteed.

Secondly, at least in this case, it might be beneficial to **BECOME PART OF THE SYSTEM.** Despite its size, this is a system that works based upon representation. In this case, your vote really does count. The truth is that whoever is running the HOA, as well as the property manager, if there is one, lives in genuine fear of losing power and with it, perks.

For example, I was once involved in a case that dealt with a property manager who engaged in, to be kind, questionable tactics. Furniture and property were removed from rental units and placed in other units, which were then billed for "new" fixtures or furniture

The keys to units were given to family and friends of the property manager, who stayed free and without the knowledge or consent of the owner. In a few cases, units were rented and the money simply pocketed, outright theft.

My own client had become red in the face trying to deal with the property manager, who was arrogant and belligerent. He had been told that there was no way he could get out of his rental agreement, and that the property manager would do whatever he wanted with the condominium whenever he wanted, just not in those words.

Fortunately, he had this on tape. First, we went to the web site for the property management company, to check the date of the next HOA meeting. There it was, describing the event so that it sounded more like a party; with food, a live mariachi band, etc.

There was an open invitation for anyone with business that day to address the HOA members. We sent a tape of his conversation with my client to the property manager, and advised him that we intended to attend the HOA meeting, play it for the members, and move for the removal of the property management group. He was released from his contract the next day.

You might also consider actually running for office in the HOA. The time commitment is nowhere near as demanding as you might expect, unless you become treasurer or president. Unlike most other public offices, you do not need to promise your soul to everyone in sight and collect a huge war chest of campaign funds to play.

Even running for office unsuccessfully has its benefits. You are considered the loyal opposition, a threat to the powers that be. Therefore, they will want to keep you fat, happy, and passive, whether they acknowledge the fact or not.

It seems like an obvious point, but it is also worth mentioning that you just might not be a part of the HOA at all. If you are house, as opposed to a condominium or apartment, consider the age of your dwelling. Is it a little older than the rest of the construction that has sprung up around it?

If so, its existence might pre-date the existence of the HOA. If this is the case, get a lawyer to do a title search on you property, and review the documents that created the HOA. Unless your home has been specifically included in the HOA with the consent of yourself or a previous owner, you are probably not a member. This means that you would be exempt from dues and all of the other consequential obligations.

I suggest hiring an attorney for one additional reason. This is not a point that the local HOA will concede readily, as they will be losing revenue and power over others, the two things all forms of government crave most. Chances are that even if you are capable of doing a title examination of your property on your own, and come to the correct conclusions, your proof will be disregarded.

Instead, the typical HOA will plod along, continuing to bill for unpaid dues and using typical enforcement tactics. This could result in a foreclosure action being filed against your home, which makes for a very high stakes game of chicken. Better to play it safe and have a professional opinion in your back pocket from the outset.

For the same reason, it is best to do the simple things that can potentially avoid a conflict altogether. This would mean that, when in doubt, you bow to the authority of the HOA if in fact you are a member. When in doubt, particularly when substantial expense is involved, get consent before doing things that might cause a problem.

Most ordinarily, this would include matters such as home improvements; painting, repairs, of any signage.

You might be surprised how deeply an HOA, or a county zoning board, can care about the content and appearance of even a small sign. I live in a city that is wall to wall with miniature golf courses covered with eight foot fiberglass dinosaurs and sharks. Still, the number of hoops it takes to obtain approval for a small, innocuous road sign is amazing.

This brings us to one of the most common, and to many of us, important questions regarding an HOA. Can I keep a Pet?

I admit to being an animal lover. For years, I took my cat to work. He was big, about twenty five pounds, slow, and good natured. I would leave him in the kitchen area of the office, where he wouldn't get in the way. In fact, he usually would only come out when the client up front happened to be female. Then, he would appear and turn on the charm. Some clients would call ahead and schedule to come in on days when I expected to bring the cat.

The point is that pets become family. Nothing is worse, for example, for an elderly person than having to relocate due to health and being ordered to surrender a pet. It is heartbreaking, often unfair, and destructive for the person and the animal.

Few people know this, but there is considerable ammunition with which to fight back. In some fairly broad categories, you have an unequivocal right to keep your animal. For example:

- If you live in public housing, you have the right to a pet
- If you live in subsidized housing, and meet the definition of elderly

- or disabled, you have the right to a pet.
- If you have a service anima, you have the right to keep it with you
- If you need your animal because of a disability, you may have the right to keep it

The first two of these exceptions are provided by Federal Law. Thus, you should expect few problems if this is the case. However, keep in mind that this does not prevent your landlord from making reasonable demands. These would include cleaning up after the pet both inside and outside of your unit, and also as to where you can take your pet.

A **service animal** can be defined as an animal specifically trained to help you with a disability. The best and most common example would be a seeing- eye dog. This is the clearest, bright line exception, insomuch as the need for the animal is usually obvious and undeniable.

The next category, however, has endless shades of gray. The Americans with Disabilities Act provides that if you are disabled, and your animal in some way "helps" your disability, you may have the right to keep it regardless of the wishes of the landlord.

Unlike the service animal which performs a specified task, which can easily be observed, pinning down a definition here is about as easy as nailing Jello to a tree. For example, you might explain to your HOA that your pet helps you handle stress. You would probably receive a skeptical response from many property managers and HOA's.

However, that can be a perfectly legitimate reason to keep the pet, and produce a legally enforceable right. For example, a client of mine was diabetic, and was having difficulty controlling his blood sugar. Part of this was due to work related stress, according to his doctor. Post-traumatic stress disorder or depression are for the same reason legitimate basis.

In such cases, expect to be asked about your disability and the need for the animal. The absolutely essential thing to do is to get something in writing from your treating physician describing your condition and the need for the pet. Chances are that this will satisfy whoever is doing the questioning. Keep a copy of the document in your files, as the problem could repeat itself if property management of your unit changes hands.

The HOA is generally within its rights to do the following:

1. Require proof from a licensed medical doctor of the resident's disability if it is not apparent, and of the need for a service or comfort animal.

2. If your state allows, ask for information on how the animal has been trained to assist with the disability.

3. If the service or comfort animal exceeds the weight limit of your pet policy,

Ask for a letter from the medical doctor confirming that this specific dog or type of dog is required. While the animal may be required, it is considered a working animal and not a pet; therefore, that specific animal may not be needed to assist the disabled individual.

4. It is reasonable to require the resident to be in control of and in the company of the service animal whenever present in common areas.

5. It is also reasonable to require the owner to control the animal in accordance with noise and

nuisance rules, and to be responsible for any damage caused byt the animal to any common area.

If you do not already have the pet, get a copy of the pet policy from your housing authority and review it. Whether or not the policy is in compliance with the Federal Fair Housing Act, it is safe to say that at least parts of it will be applicable to you and your situation.

It is also advisable to go ahead and discuss the situation with the property manager, although you might want to have your legal proof in order before doing so depending on the level of resistance. In most situations, it will be difficult to impossible to conceal an animal from property management for long, and the act of concealment can make the interaction all the more difficult.

Most cities have laws that regulate the number and kind of animals that you can own. If you intend to purchase, or already possess, something more exotic than a dog or cat, it would be wise to familiarize yourself with the local laws.

Also be aware that the Americans with Disabilities Act is applicable to cases where a "comfort pet" is helpful to a condition. As discussed earlier, this can include mental and emotional disorders. It is worth knowing that if your rights under the act have been violated, you can sue.

Chapter Eight

How Much Can You Bite Off

And How Much Should You Chew

A disturbing trend in the past few years is the rising cost, in both money and time, of going to court. In some ways, this has to do with the increasing complexity of our day to day lives. However, in others, there is the unmistakable sign of a movement to run the little guy out of the courtroom.

This has been accomplished by increasing costs and simultaneously limiting access. For example, several years ago, major financial players such as credit card companies and health care providers began inserting mandatory arbitration clauses in their contracts.

Of course, as they would explain, nobody can be compelled to sign whatever agreement they offer up. In reality, however, few even bother to read the lengthy and confusing documents presented to them when they are making a major decision, such as buying a home or car, or worse yet, planning a major surgery. Even if they do, the situations do not lend themselves to comfort in negotiation, or even to asking reasonable questions.

This has been going on for some time. Several years ago, I was approached by a couple who had planned a romantic honeymoon cruise, and instead experienced the honeymoon from hell.

This is the story. A few months before the wedding, the husband booked a discount cruise of the Caribbean, setting sail the morning after the wedding. That left one day for the flight to Miami where they were scheduled to board.

Things went smoothly for a time. They got to the dock early, with plenty of time to review the necessary paperwork before boarding. This is where they made their mistake.

Hard to call what happened a mistake, actually. These were two people about to embark on a dream trip, and one of the single, happiest moments of their lives. They were handed a big envelope full of glossy photographs of exotic locals and exciting things to do. At the bottom of the stack, on pale, inconspicuous parchment was something more important.

This was the paperwork that had to be signed before boarding. It was about eight pages long to their recollection, with lots of small print on front and back of each page. There were spaces at the margin for them to put their initials by some major provisions.

The customer service representative for the cruise line helpfully guided them through the paperwork, pointing out all of the places where they needed to put their initials and showing them where to sign and date the document. Unlike most vacationers, who are too caught up in the moment to read the document or question, the husband did ask a few cursory questions about the document before signing.

It was just paperwork, industry standard, they were told. This was more or less true, but the answer was not responsive to the question. What was never discussed, disclosed, or even noticed was a paragraph buried in the lower, middle portion of page six of the document. It read as follows:

It is agreed that any claim against service provider (I.E. CRUISE LINE) and

buyer shall be resolved by mandatory mediation, which must be requested

in writing within thirty (30) days of the conclusion of services (I.E. THE CRUISE)

or all right to recovery is forever and irrevocably waived.

It is also understood that any mediation or dispute resolution action (I.E. COURT CASE)

brought against provider is within the exclusive jurisdiction of courts of the State of

Florida and of Dade County.

There was a short signature space at the left margin by this clause, which they had initialed ask they had been instructed to do. The print was small, but the at least some of the language was in bold print.

This can be important when arguing the fairness of a contract, or a clause in a contract. The principle generally resolves around the issue of whether a reasonable person would have noticed and understood the language in question.

These words became more important in light of later events. Two days into the cruise, the bride and groom had dinner on the ship. Everything was delicious, except for the creamy soup, which the wife said tasted a little off. Based on her advice, her husband skipped the soup and went directly to the main course.

About four hours later, she was violently sick. There was a nurse on board, but no doctor. She was told that she had some kind of stomach virus, and that she would have to wait the thing out. She was offered fluids, but unable to take them. The situation went on for two more days, during which time she was received no further medical care.

When the ship finally docked in Miami, she had lost several pounds, and was severely dehydrated. They had already arranged a rental car for the return home to South Carolina. She continued to be sick through the day and half journey home, checking into the hospital immediately upon arrival.

By the time I met them, thirty days had already passed. It took a while for her to recover, and longer to complete the settling in process which results from a move. They still had a copy of the paperwork they had signed on the dock, but neither recalled reading the agreement.

This would have been a difficult case under the best of circumstances. From her account, it seemed likely that what happened to her was the result of food poisoning. To collect, we would have had to prove that theory out, which is done through lab tests. When she was at sea, no lab tests were performed. At the hospital several days later, they had only treated symptoms, leaving us with no proof. Nevertheless, it might have been possible to win a lawsuit based upon her testimony, especially if we could have found other passengers who had the same experience.

Alas, it was over before it started. It turned out that the limitations on liability in the contract were ironclad. There was even a United States Supreme Court case which upheld the restrictions, which to me and probably most other people seemed grossly unfair. I began to wonder if the Justices had a private industry provided cruise ship at their beck and call, or some kind of free pass.

Sadly, the husband had not had time to put the wife on his insurance. The result was that two nice people started their lives together with an unexpected five figure medical bill, all of which had to be paid right out of their pockets.

`Since then, such clauses have spread like a rash. There are reasons for this, and many of them are rational. Usually, they involve judicial economy; in other words, lowering the cost of the judicial system. Fine a goal as this is, we all know how much interest government has in controlling its spending in any other setting, so hard to buy this as the primary reason.

More likely it has to do with skepticism on the part of big business and government when it comes to juries deciding things. The trend is to make it oppressively expensive or impossible, to have your dispute resolved by a jury of your peers. The litigation system now filters out those with minor disputes or limited resources, so only the big boys frequent the court system, unless they feel the need to take you there.

When they do, the average citizen feels a boot to his throat well before any trial date. The rules are designed to move cases along in ways that require sophisticated players, who have familiarity with their limited group of peers, and the process. Anyone and anything else is seen as a nuisance or an intrusion.

This situation has nothing to do with government. However, it translates well as an example. There are many situations in which statutes or administrative rules prevent an individual from bringing an action against the state, severely limit recovery, or raise the difficulty level of the process well beyond the comfort level of most people.

For example, in order to bring an action for wrongful discharge or employment discrimination, it is first necessary to request a federal investigation of the alleged wrongful conduct, or one by the comparable state agency. The process tends to be lengthy and the agencies unresponsive, at least after the initial flurry of activity.

This changes toward the end, however. At that point, the complaining party is issued what is known as a "Right to Sue" letter. As you might expect, the letter serves as an authorization to file a lawsuit in Federal or State court. It usually arrives six months to a year from the date at which the investigation was begun.

However, the complaining party is given nowhere near that leisurely amount of time in which to act. The deadline is ninety days from the mailing date at which the letter was mailed. If you are trying to find a lawyer, or raise the necessary money to pursue a case, this is not much time.

In other situations, the cause of action is not barred, but the expenses are stratospheric and frontloaded so that it is impossible to get into the game without serious money. For example, many states require an expert witness to be retained, and to file an accompanying affidavit, when a medical or legal malpractice case is filed. Few in either profession wish to be a pariah among their peers, so the handful who are willing to testify offer their services to a captive market, at artificially inflated prices.

Once this has been accomplished, things only get worse. In the past few years, the Federal Rules of Procedure regarding discovery have been rewritten, in a subtle way that is hardly noticeable on a casual reading. Nevertheless, the consequences of failing to understand the significance of the change can be catastrophic, especially for those brave enough to litigate *pro se* (in order words, to act as their own attorney).

The heart of the issue is addressed in Federal Rule 37, under the Title "Motion for Order Compelling Disclosure or Discovery. For purposes of this discussion, we will first review the Rule in its entirety. The points which most merit discussion will be in bold print.

TITLE V. DISCLOSURES AND DISCOVERY.

(a) MOTION FOR AN ORDER COMPELLING DISCLOSURE OR DISCOVERY.

(1) In General. On notice to other parties and all affected persons, a party may move for an order compelling disclosure or discovery. The motion must include a certification that he movant has in good faith

conferred or attempted to confer with the person or party failing to make disclosure or discovery in an effort to obtain it without court action.

(2) Appropriate Court. A motion for an order to a party must be made in the court where the action is pending...

(4) **Evasive or Incomplete Disclosure, Answer, or Response. For purposes of this subdivision (a)** *an evasive or incomplete disclosure, answer, or response must be treated as a failure to disclose, answer, or respond.*

(5) Payment of expenses, Protective Orders.

(A) If the Motion is Granted **(or disclosure or discovery is provided after filing). If the motion is granted-or if the disclosure or requested discovery is provided after the motion is filed-***the court must, after giving an opportunity to be heard, require the party or deponent whose conduct necessitated the motion, the party or attorney advising the conduct, or both to pay the movant's reasonable expenses incurred in making the motion, including attorney's fees. But the court must not order payment if:*

(i) the movant filed the motion before attempting in good faith to obtain the disclosure or discovery without court action.

(ii) the party's non-disclosure, response, or objection was substantially justified; or

(iii) other circumstances make an award of expenses unjust.

This sounds fair enough on the face of it. The exchange of information prior to trial is the single factor that most insures a just result. Failure to respond to discovery requests, or to answer questions in a deposition in an open and honest fashion, causes unnecessary delays and expenses to all parties involved.

The problem lies in what the Federal Court system has become. Once, discovery requests could be anticipated to include a dozen or so standard questions. They were of the sort that any person of reasonable intelligence could respond to, at nominal expense.

Unfortunately, that is no longer the case. It is typical for the Plaintiff in a Federal lawsuit to receive hundreds of pages of discovery requests. A complete response can require the collection of detailed information not in the possession of the party, or documents he or she does not possess, such as medical records.

Bad as that sounds, it only gets worse. Guess who gets to decide if your answers to the questions are sufficient? Or whether you have produced all of the right documents? You guessed it, the opposing lawyer.

The Rules more or less require the court to Court to impose sanctions if the judge agrees that the responses were not timely (completed within twenty to thirty days) and complete, there is a huge incentive to put this issue before the court. Sanctions can include such things as the outright dismissal of a case, the dismissal of a cause of action, or at the very least, an award of attorney's fees and costs of the motion. In some cases, that can be a tidy sum, well into the four or five figure range.

In reality, few Plaintiffs have the capacity to respond to many of the questions that will be thrown at them. Sometimes, even more gratingly, the Plaintiff will be asked to provide information that the Defendant could easily obtain, and almost certainly already has.

For example, I once represented a Plaintiff who was arrested on questionable charges, held for days without bond, and subject to a physical beating by officers. Defense counsel asked for a criminal history of the Plaintiff, who was over seventy years old, had lived in several states, and had a failing memory.

Since Defense counsel represented the county and the arresting officer, getting this information was a snap. They were tied into the federal system, which included all federal and state records for anyone with a social security number. Nevertheless, they filed a motion demanding that my client untangle his legal history for them, something virtually impossible for him to do.

Even the more gently disposed of judges will grant an award of costs in such a situation, albeit that he not require payment of the costs until such time as the case is resolved. This is still a nice set off against any award that the Plaintiff might obtain when and if the case goes to a jury. If he or she cannot afford to pay the costs, there is the real possibility of serving jail time for contempt of court.

If you are going to court, it is important to give serious thought to two questions. The first is what is the most advantageous place for your case to be heard? The second is how do I keep it there?

Just like a poker game, you will find that the person with limited resources should think hard before playing for big stakes. This may seem unfair, but they will be faced with an intricate legal process designed for a sophisticated, intimate group of players. In other words, strangers are not welcome.

This might be merely discouraging. However, when that borderline hostile process is combined with rules that actually require the court to impose monetary sanctions in many situations, there is a lot to be worried about.

Without specific information about a case, it is difficult to impossible to determine its value. However, it is possible to at least possible to identify some of the factors that go into making that determination. Among them are:

1. Actual Damages: This is the value of whatever the Plaintiff has lost. This can typically include medical bills, lost revenue, wages or business opportunity, destroyed or damaged property, or whatever else could arguably be counted as value towards putting the Plaintiff back where he would be if the incident in question had never happened. These are sometimes referred to as "hard damages". The insurance industry puts the most emphasis on this sort of damage when evaluating a claim, since these things are easy to assign a dollar value to, and usually impossible to deny where they exist at all.

The category of actual damages also includes things which are clearly compensable but more difficult to place a value on. These can include pain and suffering where a person is injured, loss of enjoyment of life, and loss of consortium, which means the damage that a husband or wife suffers in being forced to care for an injured spouse, or in being otherwise deprived of the benefits of the relationship.

The value of these types of damages is usually determined by a judge, jury, or arbitrator, essentially based upon their own personal values and their reaction to the testimony of the Plaintiff. It has been my experience that the Plaintiff will generally place a higher value on these kinds of damages than an independent third party will. It is hard to walk a mile in another man's shoes, and sadly, many people will not even try.

2. **Punitive Damages:** Punitive damages are seldom awarded, and not even an issue in most civil cases. The theory behind punitive damages is that the conduct of the defendant was so bad, ill spirited, and destructive that an award of actual damages is insufficient. There should also be an award of additional money meant to "punish" the defendant and to send a signal that society will not tolerate the behavior in question.

The value of punitive damages is a case is a matter of pure speculation. However, in the infrequent cases in which it is awarded, a verdict for punitive damages can often exceed the value of the actual damages claim by a considerable margin.

So how do we get an idea of the value of the case? Unfortunately, the process is more art than science. There are an endless number of factors which go into determining the value of a lawsuit for settlement or trial. Some of them are easy to assign a dollar amount to, many are not. Some go completely unnoticed, such as the whether a certain member of the jury didn't like your facial tick.

For purposes of choosing where to file a case, we can set some hard and fast rules however. Completely disregard punitive damages, which are a long shot in even the best of scenarios. Then, determine the actual damages value with this simple formula:

1. Include all actual out of pocket expenses as damages. This will include medical bills, lost wages or revenue from a business, repair or replacement of property, etc. There is an old legal term which has aged so well because of its utility; "make the Plaintiff whole." If an out of

pocket expense was or will be necessary to do this, there is a legitimate claim that the expense in question can be considered as damages.

However, there are limitations. Some expenses which might appear to be compensable damages might be difficult to justify as same. For example, if you had medical expenses for ongoing treatment of a prior condition following an accident, such as diabetes care, this might not be compensable. It would be your burden in court to prove that the medical care was required as a result of your injuries (for a reason such as elevated blood sugars as a result of your injuries.)

The same kind of theory can apply to other damages. For example, you might request compensation for lost revenue from a business contract you were unable to perform; and have the claim denied because you were found to be actually able to do some or all of the work, or had partners or employees who could have done the work instead.

The best you can do is to be honest about whether you consider an item of damages to be legitimate. Later on, somebody other than you will make the call, permanently, if only you go far enough with your case. Then apply this simple formula:

1. Start with your figure for actual damages with an assigned dollar value.

2. If your case involved pain and suffering, loss of enjoyment of life, or others of the more difficult to evaluate types of actual damages, add no more than an equal amount to the first figure. If you believe that your experience in this area was more moderate, assign a lower value.

The resulting number will not be, and is not intended to be, an accurate valuation of your claim. It is merely a yardstick which should allow you to make certain decisions. It should allow you to make an objective decision as to where to file your claim, and just how much time and effort to put into it.

Here are some generally sound rules.

1. Do not file a lawsuit in Federal District Court if the value you calculate for the claim is less than fifty thousand dollars. If you do choose to proceed in the Federal system, retain an attorney. Under no circumstances should you go forward on a pro se basis.

2. If the value you attribute to the claim is less than fifty thousand dollar but more than ten thousand dollars, consider filing the claim in the state court that handles cases in this value range. You

will find that the state court system is more user friendly, and have far fewer traps for the inexperienced or unwary. However, it is still possible to do a great deal of damage to your case in a short period of time, so I recommend hiring an attorney.

3. If the value of your case is below ten thousand, you might want to consider filing an action in small claims court. This is the most user friendly forum, where judges and support staff are used to dealing with private citizens who are handling their own claims. The potential recovery will be limited, but the process is faster, less time consuming, and more expensive.

4. If the case is worth less than ten thousand dollars, and particularly if it is worth substantially less than this figure, consider whether filing an insurance claim is a viable alternative. Your time and money might not be well spent based upon the limited potential recovery.

While you are deciding upon the right venue in which to file your case, you might also consider the issue of how to keep it there. There are situations in which it is possible for a defendant to remove a case from the court in which it was initially filed, and send it elsewhere. When this is done, it is always for strategic reasons.

A case can be removed to federal court based on diversity. A case is considered "diverse" when all of the parties bringing a lawsuit are from a different state or nation than all of the parties who are being sued. For example, if you are a citizen of California, and sue a citizen of Arizona, that person would have the right to remove the case to Federal Court, provided that you are suing for an amount of money equal or in excess to the jurisdictional limit for Federal District Court.

For reasons already discussed in this chapter, you might not want the case to be heard in Federal Court. There would be two ways to prevent this. The first would be to specify the amount of money you wish to recover in the case, and make this amount less than the jurisdictional limit for federal court. If the value of the case is less than that amount, there would be no harm in doing so.

The second would be to include a non-diverse defendant in the case. It is important to keep in mind that there are consequences to involving a person or entity in a lawsuit, and if there is no good faith reason for forcing them to participate and defend, sanctions are possible. However, if there is a valid basis to do so, adding a defendant from the same state in which you do business or reside could keep you out of federal court.

As to the various state courts, jurisdictional lines are generally drawn based upon the amounts in dispute. If you wish to avoid a higher court, for reasons of cost or otherwise, the remedy is to specify the amount of money you wish to recover in your pleadings.

CONCLUSION

Can you really get government off your back in these days and times? Not entirely, but you still can to a surprising extent. The secret, if there is one, involves lifestyle choices made well before there is an actual adversarial problem to deal with. It is a matter of limiting the "trigger points" that cause friction between yourself and whatever entity seeks to control your behavior.

If you own a business for example, you constantly make choices that will produce, or limit government involvement. Where you locate the physical shop, whether, who, and when you hire, and the nature of the business all have a major impact.

Likewise, your choice of the state, county, and even the street address at which you live will have a considerableeffect. It goes without saying that there is a wide discrepancy in the rate at which states and communities choose to tax their citizens. The same is true with regards to civil penalties such as child support. The minutiae of government can often be the most ego driven, irrational, and destructive part.

Part of a successful approach is to simply understand what can and cannot be taxed. For example, you might find that the life logic taught to you by earlier generations no longer applies. Why wreck your health and squander your youth on high stress, seventy hour work weeks, when the fruits of your labor are inevitably redistributed to strangers who do little or nothing? Your time in this world is finite, indeterminate, and irreplaceable. Reclaiming at least some of it for yourself or your loved ones is a tremendous benefit. Better yet, nobody has figured out how to redistribute that, at least so far.

The End.